SEX PRIESTESS

Liberate your Eros, Embody your Feminine
Power & Become a Force for Awakening

By Nadine Lee

First published in 2023 by Nadine Lee
©Nadine Lee

The moral rights of the author have been asserted.

This book is an Inspirational Book Writers book.

Author: Lee, Nadine

Title: Sex Priestess; Liberate your Eros, Embody your Feminine Power & Become a Force for Awakening

ISBN: 9798375874616

All rights reserved. Except as permitted under the Australian Copyright Act 1968 (for example, a fair dealing for the purposes of study, research, criticism or review), no part of this book may be reproduced, stored in a retrieval system, communicated or transmitted in any form or by any means without prior written permission. All enquiries should be made to the author at *nadine@tantricalchemy.net*

Editor-in-chief: Rachel Koontz
Cover Design: Sarah Rose Graphic Design

Disclaimer:

The material in this publication is of the nature of general professional advice, but it is not intended to provide specific guidance for particular circumstances and it should not be relied on as the basis for any decision to take action or not take action on any particular matter which it covers. Readers should obtain individual advice from the author where appropriate, before making any such decision. To the maximum extent permitted by law, the author and publisher disclaim all responsibility and liability to any person, arising directly or indirectly from any person taking or not taking action based on the information in this publication.

Tables of Contents

Introduction: Meeting The Sex Priestess v
Chapter 1: Reawakening The Goddess 1
Chapter 2: My Story/Herstory 9

★ ★ ★

Code 1: Opening The Womb Portal 31
Code 2: The Divine Masculine 53
Code 3: Inner Union 81
Code 4: Self-Sourced Eros 103
Code 5: Orgasmic Co-Creation 141
Code 6: Initiatrix Of Awakening 165
Code 7: Living As The Sex Priestess 193
End Note 209
Resources/Appendix 211

INTRODUCTION

Meeting the Sex Priestess

There is a deep knowing in my womb and heart of a time in history when woman, and especially her body and sexuality, was honored as sacred.

I have memories in my cells of times when women would dance in temples and men would come and worship them.

These women were highly trained sex priestesses who possessed the ability to unlock the healing and liberating energy of the feminine in any man or woman who came into their temples.

This feminine energy was *Shakti*, pure life force, symbolized by the serpent—the kundalini energy as the expression of transformation, awakening, purification and enlightenment.

These priestesses worked to awaken this energy within themselves first and foremost, and were then able to awaken it within others through their divine presence, dance, healing arts, and sacred touch. They knew how to use the energy of sexuality to heal and awaken. They were the healers, the oracles, the guardians of the sacred, the dancing dakinis, the pure vessels of divine feminine energy. They would bleed freely and the sight of blood on their garments was seen as holy. It was considered an utter privilege to be in the presence of that sacred elixir.

This was a time when feminine sexuality was respected and revered, rather than hidden in the shadows and cast away as taboo. During this time in history, these women acted as the gatekeepers of an ancient wisdom that was stored deep within their wombs. They were not afraid of the wisdom they held; they knew and trusted it intimately, and they felt safe to express and use it to awaken and heal humanity, and to support the evolution of consciousness.

These memories have resurfaced many times along my own journey of awakening the Feminine Energy within myself. Every time I speak about them or write about them, I feel an expansive energy coursing through my body. Sometimes I also feel a contraction, because the power of this energy humbles me. It is great beyond measure, and with great power comes great responsibility.

The sex priestess is an archetypal figure in the collective consciousness of humanity. She is the part of you that—just as she once did in the temples—dances through life (literally and metaphorically) as an open receptive channel transmitting truth, beauty, liberation and freedom. She does this simply through the power of her embodied transmission. She does this simply by living her truth, speaking her truth and expressing her truth through all she chooses to create. Therefore, the way this archetype is expressed looks different for every single woman on the planet. She is the untamed force of creation itself.

In order to become this open vessel of creation, she must go through a process of unraveling all that is in the way of being open to receive; everything that blocks her from being the portal of creation. The unraveling process starts with undoing all her societal, religious, and familial conditioning around being a woman, specifically around a woman's body and sexuality.

She is what we would call an *illuminated one*, an enlightened one, and not in the traditional sense of a guru sitting above others. Rather, she is an illuminated one in the truly embodied, integrated sense—a human who has fully activated their fullest potential by merging their sexuality with their spirituality. Thus this individual is able to anchor spiritual information through the physical body, through their sexuality, into creations on this earth plane. She is not looking to escape to nirvana. She is very much here and now, present to the human experience while simultaneously connected to a power beyond herself. Her consciousness is expanded yet her feet are firmly anchored on the ground. A priestess has mastered dancing the worlds. She does not see living in a suburban family home as less sacred and holy than living in a temple or ashram. She knows the true secret of tantra: that everything is sacred, and that we are very much here to anchor spirit into matter. This must be accomplished through a healed and awakened sexuality. For when we deny our sexuality and our bodies—as so many religious and spiritual teachings teach us to do—we are severing ourselves from the true and real definition of the word 'enlightenment'.

The sex priestess is the fully empowered woman; unstoppable, charismatic and unapologetic about who she is and what feels right for her. She swims in a sea of authenticity and creative fire. She is lit from within. When you meet her, when you make eye contact with her–you remember that you are these things too. She reminds you of your wildness and your truth. She becomes a catalyst for your liberation by reigniting your inner flame within. Stand in her presence, and you will walk away forever changed.

Throughout history, the sex priestess has had many different expressions. She has been called a *Devadasi* (temple dancer) in

Indian traditions, a dancing *Dakini* in the Tibetan Buddhist lineage, a temple dancer, an exotic dancer, a sacred prostitute, a tantrika, a performer – essentially, she is any woman who has fully awakened to her full sexual and erotic expression and knows how to use that sacred energy to awaken others. She does not necessarily do this by engaging with them sexually. She awakens others through the power of her own beingness. Simply by others witnessing her in her full feminine power, whether that be performing onstage captivating an audience with her embodied movements or simply sharing her presence.

Isis, Mary Magdalen, and the Sex Priestess through History

The archetype of the sex priestess has been hidden from our history books, but she can be found in all of the world's spiritual traditions. Sex priestesses and sacred temple prostitutes could be found across the ancient world, from India to Egypt to Babylon. In the ruins of many ancient temples, you can still find small sacred brothel rooms outside the main temple where worthy worshippers could receive sexual initiations from highly trained priestesses.

Wise women like Mary Magdalen held the knowledge of these powerful rites and initiation. Magdalen, the first disciple of Jesus who was later denounced by the church as a whore, is one of the most well-known and powerful historical archetypal embodiments of the sex priestess. She is an aspect of all of our psyches that has been largely dismissed, misunderstood and cast into the collective unconscious. As the feminine polarity awakens and revives on the planet, her archetype plays a large role in unlocking the disowned and shamed parts of our sexual psyche, individually and of course collectively. For as we do the inner work on our individual self, we effectively contribute to liberating the collective consciousness at large. In the book *Magdalen Manuscripts,* a channeled rendition of Mary Magdalen's role as a highly trained Sex Priestess in the Temples of Isis, one of the authors channels Mary Magdalen, who recounts the story of her and Jesus (Yeshua)'s love. The Mary Magdalen of that book tells us that she was an advanced initiate in the temple of Isis in Egypt, which was a cult of women who were highly trained in the tantric arts and sex magic. The Goddess Isis was known as a great magician. She had the most *heka* (the creative energy of the universe) of all the gods, and even the magic god Thoth called her the *Mistress of Magic*. Magic was not used to manipulate matter but rather to reach the very Source, to correct what was obviously wrong or spoiled. One of the main practices of these highly trained Sex Priestesses in the Cult of Isis was indeed sex magic. If you read between the lines of some Gnostic sources, it very much appears that there was something akin to *sex magic* in Egypt. And even before Isis, there is evidence that her Sumerian predecessor Inanna and her priestesses definitely performed sexual rituals. This magic was kept secret for fear of its falling into the wrong hands, being accessed by people who would not use it for their spiritual advancement but rather for their own often selfish means or to harm others. In a sense, the same can be said about tantra and awakening the powerful force of sexuality in general. It has to be in the right hands. In order to handle it responsibly, the person awakening this energy must be well aware of how powerful it truly is and must have undergone some serious inner alchemy of their sexual shadows and especially their relationship to power.

In the *Magdalen Manuscripts*, the author channels Mary Magdalen's story of how the disciples judged her to be a whore because she had a gold bracelet of Isis on her arm, signifying her initiation into secret sexual mysteries. After that meeting, she actually practices a form of sexual magic with Yeshua (an equivalent of tantra, but with Egyptian terminology) to increase his *ka* (energetic body) and prepare him for his final ordeal of death and resurrection.

This book, which I highly recommend, is just one of many accounts of the sacred sexual knowledge attributed to Mary Magdalen—and she is only one of many wise women through the ages who held the knowledge of sacred sexual rites. Recently, scholars of religion have been unearthing a deep secret hidden within the church for centuries: that early Christian rituals such as the Eucharist likely involved sacred sex. These powerful practices were driven underground to keep the power out of the hands of the people and to maintain the total authority of male priests. The rest is history.

But today, what I know in my womb is increasingly being revealed as truth: the fact that at one time, sex and spiritual worship were not separate. From ancient Egypt to tantric Buddhism to early Taoism to early Christianity, sexuality has been a part of our understanding of the sacred—and women known as sex priestesses have been the holders of this profound and secret wisdom.

My Own Journey to the Priestess

I believe the sex priestess has always been alive in me, since as I was as young as six years old, questioning the existence of God and a higher power while simultaneously establishing a connection to my orgasm and the power of eros. I have always been hungry for answers to the big questions: *Who am I? Why am I here?* My fascination with the nature of the self and reality has been a driving force behind everything I do. At age 14, I experienced a spiritual awakening that changed me forever, and again at 21, I experienced another awakening when I was ready to truly walk the path of the sex priestess as an embodied way of life and my life's work. It was then, at 21, that my first teachers and yoga and tantra found me.

As cliche as it sounds, I feel that I didn't choose this path, but rather the path chose me. In fact, as I will share in later chapters, I resisted this path for so many reasons. To truly walk the path of a sex priestess is to walk the path of truth. This requires tremendous amounts of courage, as you step outside of the status quo. You must die to everything that you thought you were to discover who you truly are. When we begin to awaken our sexuality and merge that with our spirituality is when we begin to truly unlock our gifts and our truth. This is essentially the illuminated path. It is not some special path assigned to gurus and meditating yogis in caves – this is a path every single human being is invited to embark upon. However, it is up to every individual whether they will answer the call and walk the path or stay enslaved in a path carved out for them by someone else.

A Journey of Unraveling and Opening

When most people hear the term sex priestess, they will automatically jump to thinking that this is a book about how to have great sex. This also tends to happen when people hear the term 'tantra'. Ask anyone what they think tantra is and they will almost always automatically jump to it being all about sex. However, the truth is that both the path of a sex priestess and the path of tantra (which, in my view, are interchangeable) are of course inclusive of sex, but sex is the by-product of something much deeper that must be established first. We experience the fruits of amazing sex after we extract the weeds and dead debris within us—meaning, the conditioning of the mind, negative habitual thought patterns and stagnant emotions associated with unresolved traumas that are stored in the body. Before opening to this immense power that is our sexual energy, we must clear out our physical and emotional vessels, so that the life force can flow through us. This is what enables great sex, creativity and a deepening of our spiritual connection. We simply cannot work with this powerful force if we are a clogged pipe full of mental, emotional and physical blockages.

So this journey we are about to embark on—the journey of embodying the sex priestess archetype—is one of unravelling and setting the foundations. Sexuality is a powerful and advanced energy, and we must start the journey with the body, specifically learning to feel safe, grounded and present in one's body. Because an average two out of three women on this planet have experienced some level of sexual abuse or trauma, there is an epidemic of disembodiment as a result of a trauma response that we must address. This path of healing and embodiment is not a linear path. It is a journey through many layers of the self. I have been doing this work for 15 years, and I still have to come back to process further trauma through my body on a regular basis. The layers just keep revealing themselves. It is like an onion that peels back layer after layer. It's not about digging for new things to examine, but rather being patient and holding compassion along the path of growth and evolution. The path of embodiment is the path of the feminine, and as you will learn, the feminine takes time to open and unravel – she is a great mystery and she is spiralic in nature, not linear. We must be prepared for any and all unexpected detours that life takes us on. This is not a path of quick fix or disillusionment. The path of tantra is one of embracing one's humanity fully, which is often messy. It is about being completely present to the human experience in order to fulfill our spiritual assignments. This means being fully embodied so we can anchor what our higher selves came here to create in this third-dimension, earthly experience.

The Path Ahead

I have charted the path of this journey ahead as a road map to unlocking the sex priestess within you and guiding you along your own tantric path of embodiment and empowerment. Outlined in this book are what I believe and have had embodied experience living the seven codes of unlocking the sex priestess within you. A *code* is simply one core aspect of the embodiment process. Each code is something that gets unlocked within you, in no particular linear way at all; and not in some confined timeline, either. In fact, these codes could unlock in a completely different order than what I've laid out for you. The important thing to note is that there is no right or wrong place to begin this journey. You are here now and I encourage you to keep an open mind and heart throughout this journey. As you make your way through each code, you will experience your own awakenings and embodied remembrances along the way. Listen to this always.

The first code is *Opening the Womb Portal*. We begin by finding our true power through connecting with the power of the womb and releasing the trapped emotions stored in the body. This descent is one that each of us must summon the courage to take, making our first steps to reclaim the temple that is our bodies—a space which we may have abandoned or shamed for many years, decades or even lifetimes.

The second code is *The Divine Masculine*, where we dive deep into integrating and healing your relationship to the masculine. A Sex Priestess—an empowered integrated woman—must have a healthy relationship to the masculine, as it is expressed in both the men in her life and her own inner masculine. If she wants to be in union with herself and in healthy partnership, this work is the essential foundation.

The third code, *Inner Union*, is all about creating harmony within yourself through inner union of the masculine and feminine energies. This union of opposites is also the highest stage of the alchemical process and the ultimate goal of alchemy, for one truly liberates themselves beyond duality and into oneness consciousness.

The fourth code, *Self-Sourced Eros*, is about reclaiming all parts of your sexuality as a woman and releasing those parts that still source fulfillment, pleasure and love from outside of yourself (partners, lovers, recognition from men, success, validation or any other external source). Here, we'll explore how to start sourcing ourselves from within. This is such a powerful code of the Sex Priestess, and one that required me to learn and unlearn old behaviours and patterns so that I could truly be the source my own pleasure and bliss.

We are ready for the fifth code, *Orgasmic Co-Creation*, once we have started circulating our sexual energy through the work of the previous codes. Now it is time to learn how to harness this energy into co-creation with life itself. We will explore the unlimited possibilities available to us once we are aware of how to harness this potent force within. So it is one thing to learn how to activate our sexual energy as a Sex Priestess, but the next evolution of that is learning how to channel this energy into our creativity and everything that we came here to birth.

The sixth code, *Initiatrix of Awakening*, teaches us how to begin to extend our inner life force to penetrate every inch of our reality. Once this energy is unlocked and fully activated in a woman, she naturally embodies her inner Sex Priestess and begins to become a healing and transformational force for others. When this code is unlocked, the Sex Priestess is activated not only in lovemaking, but in every interaction with men.

Simply being in her presence activates his eros and she knows how to support the alchemy of this energy for awakening.

The seventh and final code is *Living as the Sex Priestess*, which is the full-circle coming home and integration of all the lessons we learn along our healing path. It is about establishing how these translate into shaping our soul's work or our dharma in our lifetime. This code is about the journey of integration after you have answered the soul call to heal yourself, look at your sexual shadows, reclaim the exiled parts of yourself, face your core wounds and find your power through this process. It is the necessary reflection after you go on a wild journey, gaining so much wisdom along your path—only to find herself back to where it all began, yet the lens through which you perceive the world has shifted radically as your internal world has come to a place of peace, wholeness and integration. And from this place you fully reclaim your power, and extend your wisdom outwards by supporting others along their own soul journeys.

CHAPTER 1

REAWAKENING THE GODDESS

This time in history I recall is known as the Goddess culture. It is very ancient, tracing back to the Egyptian temples and and across pre-Christian Europe. The earliest goddess figurines found by archeologists, depicting lush and curved female forms, date back over 25,000 years. This was a time when society was matriarchal and where female sexuality was liberated and celebrated, not suppressed and cast deep into the collective unconscious and thus used as a commodity. Today we are experiencing an awakening of this sacred energy, a collective remembering of a time before patriarchal dominance of the female body and the body of the Earth. Reclaiming the sex priestess archetype is an important part of this collective awakening.

The Goddess is once again returning to balance the scales, or we are a culture dis-eased and out of balance. What we have experienced since the time of the Goddess is a drastic swinging of the pendulum into the very opposite of celebration and expression of feminine energy. Seeking to control the power of the feminine, the rise of the patriarchy is the story of the dominance, control and suppression of women's bodies, women's sexuality, and women's power—as well as the body of the earth, her wisdom and her natural resources.

The suppression of feminine energy has led us on a wild ride through history to where we are today, with the total dominance of masculine energy and values. Like all polarities in the universe, if we indulge in characteristics on the left side, we must balance them with the right side. The seesaw must be balanced to maintain equilibrium. The psyche is always seeking to create equilibrium as accurately as the body naturally balances its temperature. Eventually we get sick of dancing between extremes, and we find a middle ground. This place of balance isn't the place of muted compromise that we fear it may be. It is actually the point of union, ecstasy and harmony.

Up until the 1800s society was very far on the *conservative* side of the seesaw, as it was extremely indoctrinated by patriarchal religions which denounced the body and sexuality. The Victorian era was a time of incredible social repression where sexuality was completely shunned and hidden away. Sexuality was seen as purely private and only used for procreation of the next generation. You couldn't even say words like 'leg'—you had to use words like 'limb' to avoid calling to mind a mental image of a body part that might arouse sexual feelings. This brought sexuality into the realm of impurity through a deep-seated shame of the body itself. If you weren't having sex for the creation of God, then sex was something sinful. This created intense fear and guilt around sexuality, the body, and our natural human desires. This was reinforced by the central role of the church in culture in society, which had only two images of femininity: the pure mother (the Virgin Mary) and the dirty prostitute (Mary Magdalen).

Slowly, the pendulum began swinging the other direction at the turn of the century with the birth of psychoanalysis, when thought leaders Freud and Jung finally started to talk about sexual repression, shame around the body and disfunctional complexes around sexuality. Finally people began to consider shame of the body as a deep rooted psychological problem resulting in all sorts of unconscious fears, paranoias and repressions. If we see our body as dirty or impure, we hold this relationship to our very essence and selfhood as this. This also colors our relationship to the feminine dimension of life. The body is our connection to the feminine essence, as it is the material manifestation of our connection to mother nature, the earth, whereas the sky/cosmos is our connection to our masculine essence which is consciousness itself. This is unfortunately what all patriarchal religions have enforced—denying the body and the Earth (the feminine principle) to focus solely on consciousness and Heaven or nirvana (the masculine principle). Thinkers like Jung and Freud understood this and began to create entire bodies of work around sexual and body repression being the root of all psychological and mental disorders. This is because there is a disease, a disconnect between body, mind and spirit—the real holy trinity—which are meant to exist in harmony and wholeness. When we cut off from the body (the feminine), we experience the opposite of harmony, being dis-harmony. And the goal is to reach that middle point of equilibrium to restore true union.

In the decades following Freud and Jung came the rise of the feminists in the mid-20th century. During the feminist movement, women gained legal rights primarily to vote, which began to change the status of women who were previously as confined to their single role as housewife and child bearer, completely financially dependent upon their husband or father. Before the feminist movement, women would almost never express their feelings outwardly and if they did, other women would put them down and stop them. In America after the second world war, it was even seen as 'unpatriotic' to even be outside of the house as a woman. It wasn't until the 1960s that the second wave of feminism began, with women fighting against social confines and the limitations of jobs, expression and freedom in society as a woman. During this time the pill was introduced which lifted the shackles of motherhood for women, so women could now have sex without the risk of getting pregnant. This changed women's relationship to their sexuality completely. A sexual revolution was birthing. Women like Nancy Friday, Where Hite, Betty Friedan, Annie Sprinkle wrote books and started movements around feminine reclamation. Women were burning their bras, having sex for pleasure, voting and making their own money. They had more rights and freedom—however, they were doing it in a very masculine way. There was an unconscious anger behind liberation, which I believe had to be purged in order to cultivate harmony. The movement was driven by generations of rage about the injustices that women suffered. If we deny that suppression and the real human emotions that come with it, we do not get to heal.

This has led us to where we are today, rediscovering what awakened and liberated feminine and sexual energy actually is. What we saw in the 1960's feminist movement was a rebelling from centuries of suppression. As I mentioned earlier, when any two sides of a polarity are suppressed for too long, there is an adjustment phase where the opposed energy swings far over the other side of the pendulum, seeking balance in the middle point. What we saw during the feminist movement was women rising, yes, but they were rising by taking on their masculine qualities, not their feminine qualities. They were trying to match men and essentially to become men—they wanted to win at a man's game. There was anger, rage, resentment, fury underneath liberation. Was this true feminine power? While it was necessary for the times, it wasn't an expression of the real power women possess.

We are experiencing times now where we are again redefining and reclaiming our relationship to feminine and the power of our sexual energy that comes with it. However I believe this time in history is experiencing a softer approach towards feminism. Even using the word 'feminism' feels oppressive to me as it suggests the oppression of the feminine. These teachings of modern tantra, polarity and embodiment tap more into the essence of masculine and feminine energy, as expressed in man and woman beyond physical biology. On a deeper level, they connect us to the energetics and psychology concept of *Anima* and *Animus,* the inner masculine and feminine energies that are the real roots of imbalance and the pathways to healing. I will explore these teachings in depth throughout the book.

Where are we now? And where are we headed?

Right now feminine as an *energy* is being resurrected and redefined.

So is masculine energy.

Men and women are reclaiming their own inner masculine and feminine to heal the collective wounds of the battle of the sexes that has defined the past several thousand years of patriarchy.

We are headed in the direction we create from now. This is basic quantum physics: what we believe now is what creates our future. We are constantly creating our future through our thoughts, speech and actions.

As a woman living in these times, working alongside many others to usher in a reawakening of the goddess, I speak from the intuitive wellspring of my own experience. I will always draw upon my real life experiences throughout this book. Embodied experience is the core of the magic of the feminine. When we speak truth derived from embodied intuition and wisdom, this sparks something in others around us to then find their truth and embodied intuition and wisdom.

Finding harmony between masculine and feminine is essential to the survival of our species. We live in a paradox between logos (masculine mind) and eros (feminine heart/body). Paradox is a natural part of the human experience and everything is always balanced in pairs of opposites: day and night, masculine and feminine, positive and negative, action and stillness. The key is to always be aware of the nature of paradox, that brings us into union. This happens when we honor both sides of duality. We cannot favor one, at the expense of the other, for this is when we lose harmony and union. What we have seen though is that eros has been denied for far too long. The feminine mystery of eros, has been replaced for solely logos, mind as a way to create some sort of personal and collective control. However, as we know the law of paradox: logos without eros is incomplete. Too much of any polarity creates disharmony. In a collective mind that values logic over love and mystery, we are left dried up and dis-eased.

It is important to honor the past, where we came from. Yet I am more interested in creating the future than accepting the current reality. So where are we now? Where are you now? What is your relationship to your own feminine energy? How is your relationship to your mother, your sisters, the important women in your life? How is your relationship to nature? How is your relationship to pleasure and creativity? To your body and sexuality? I invite you to ask these very questions of yourself, to define where you are NOW, and where you want to go from here. Acknowledge your past and heal your past through telling your story in order to create our shared now and future reality. It starts now and with you.

This book is a labor of love. This book is part of my legacy to the world. A journey through my own path from sexual abuse to liberation. I believe when one woman liberates through telling her own heroine's journey, she helps others do the same. This is my intention for this book. For when we tell our story uncensored, unfiltered, and freely, we have the opportunity to liberate all these parts within ourselves and to set ourselves free. I believe it is important to tell our stories, to share the accumulated wisdom along the way; and at the same time not to let our stories define us and who we are evolving into. We all have a story. We love getting lost in a good story. In order to break free from our stories, we need to tell them so that we can liberate ourselves from the identities we've formed from them.

This is my story, this is herstory.

CHAPTER 2

MY STORY/ HERSTORY

My story is your story.

There is a herstory of women that is the collective heart and mind of the feminine. If you were drawn to this book, I know that you will see glimpses and reflections of yourself and your journey in me. In hearing my story you will understand me, and therefore understand yourself.

So who am I? How did I end up devoting my life to tantra, to guarding and reviving the ancient wisdom of the sex priestess?

This has been a journey of many lifetimes, but in this one, it begins when I was a young girl.

I remember as a child visiting graveyards and seeing the bookend of someone's life represented on a tombstone. I was always so curious, what got them there? Who was this person? What inspired them? Who loved them? What was their calling in life? Did they fall in love? How did they die? I believe the journey is much more important than the final destination, always. So before we delve into unlocking your sex priestess codes, enjoy my story and ask yourself: Where are you in your life right now? What has brought you here to this book, this moment?

Erotic innocence

The fact I was fascinated by graveyards is a pretty good indication that I was not your average child. The earliest memories I recall were choosing to play in graveyards over playgrounds. For as long as I can remember, I've been in love with all things supernatural. When I was five years old I remember sitting on the front porch with my mum and little sister in our home in Canberra, Australia after a rainstorm. We were eating our favorite grape-flavored popsicles and I was asking my mother some pretty complex questions: What happens when we die? Why do we die? Where were we before we came here? And most importantly, Who is God? And how can I meet him? I was perplexed by these questions. They consumed me and set me off on a lifelong quest for answers.

At the same time I was trying to figure out how to meet this God person, whoever he or she was, I was starting to experience all sorts of interesting sensations in my body. At six years old, I remember having my first orgasm by rubbing my clitoris on my favorite stuffed bunny, 'Rabby'. Rabby slept on my bed until I was 20 years old. He started out a fluffy white bunny gifted to me at birth and stayed with me as something of an ally/spirit animal/emotional support until my early 20s. By then, Rabby was gray, had holes in him, an eye missing, a tail about to fall off and a pretty gnarly smell. But Rabby was my first lover—I will never forget that orgasm. It was the best feeling I have ever felt and I continued to explore for years to come. At the time, I thought it was the best thing ever. I would play this pleasure game whenever I could with zero awareness of who was around me or what was going on. My mother knew what I was doing and thankfully didn't shame my exploration but rather just suggested I go into my room if I decided to explore when family friends were over.

After my obsession with wanting to know who God was, my second childhood obsession was my play dates with Rabby. I began getting curious, and I have no idea how I knew about what sex was, but shortly after beginning these explorations, I remember straight-out asking my mum, *What does sex feel like?* She was shocked, but not really surprised after witnessing my explorations. I remember her response was something along the lines of *How it feels when you play with Rabby*. I had no idea how sex worked on a practical level, but I was excited, to say the least, to learn more.

This innocent exploration of my own pleasure continued for about a year until what was about to happen would change me forever. They say sexual abuse is an initiation, because if something like this happens to you when you are young, it is your first initiation into your sexuality. Obviously it is not the ideal, moral or healthy way to be introduced to your sexuality. However I believe it puts you on the path of healing and learning to work with sexual energy as a big part of your dharma in this lifetime. This I know to be true. Little did I know that what was about to happen would initiate a whole range of emotional experiences from confusion, betrayal, pleasure, and ultimately my life's work.

My family and I were visiting a family friend's house for Christmas that year. We stayed with them in their beautiful house in the forest in the heat of Queensland, where the tropical weather, hot days and wild stormy nights always felt like my happy, safe place. It was a welcome break away from the chaos that was my family home. When we would go to family friends' houses, my parents rarely fought like they did at home. There was more stability and I felt safe, much like the feeling I had with Rabby in my bed with me every night. Total safety. Never did I consider that the source of my safety would become the source of my greatest wound.

At our family friends home was *Jake who was just seven years older than me. I loved *Jake and we always had so much fun together. He was like a big brother to me. But it seemed as though my innocent sexual explorations were vibing with his, as he was 14 years old at the time and his hormones were flying crazy. It all began as a game with him chasing me in the pool. I would swim away as fast as I could and if he caught me, he would rub my clitoris. To me, it felt just like a better version of the Rabby game I played with myself. I liked the game and didn't see anything wrong with it at the time, being the innocent and naive seven-year-old that I was. Then things got a little more private, hidden away from the eyes of others. I remember him taking showers downstairs and inviting me in after we would finish our pool 'games'. In the shower I remember being naked this time, without the protection of my bathing suit, and him rubbing my clitoris again. This time it didn't feel as pleasurable because he was more aggressive. It didn't feel like such a fun game in the shower. It wasn't painful, but I didn't really like it and of course I had no idea how to express this as a young girl.

Things began to get more and more intimate. The last memory I have of our interactions was being up in his bedroom where he would 'hump' me. We were both fully clothed and he would rub himself up and down on me, stimulating the act of sex. I thought, *Well, this must be sex.* There was zero penetration or touching of genitals but the rubbing friction under the clothes felt again like another version of the Rabby game. This time a boy twice my size was replacing rabby, so I kind of enjoyed this game also. This went on a few times, until one day his mother called out to him to open the door. I remember him freezing up and the look on his face of sheer guilt as he quickly jumped off me and pretended he was playing his video game while I lay there confused. It was at this moment that my body also froze. It was no longer a fun game. I knew that something was not right. It was at this moment, I believe, that the original shame codes got imprinted in my body. Pleasure now equaled shame, not fun play, like it used to.

I don't remember any more of these games happening after this final incident. He was so close to getting caught on top of me that I think it must have scared the shit out of him. The games stopped. I never told anyone about what happened that summer. As I got older, I realized this was not a game. It was a major violation of my boundaries as a child, and he knew exactly what he was doing as a 14-year-old boy. I held even more shame and embarrassment around the situation and I didn't want anyone to know what happened. But finally when I was 18 years old, it slipped out by accident.

For the previous years before sharing publicly what happened, I suffered intense anxiety, depression, paranoia and eating disorders—I believe as a way to cope with what happened to me when I was seven (plus another experience at 14 that left me traumatized). I remember having a breakdown to my mum, begging her to put in in a mental institution because of how fucked up I felt inside, and it just slipped out of my mouth: "I am this way because *Jake* sexually abused me when I was seven". She freaked out and I freaked out. I was so worried what repercussions this would have on *Jake*, his family and my family. Unfortunately, sexual abuse was not uncommon in our family, and I had seen what it did when every woman revealed her abuse story. In some weird way I didn't want to cause more drama in the family. This is a common pattern that victims of abuse take on, where they internalize their pain and try to prevent others from suffering from the ramifications of them speaking their truth. They don't want to become a burden, so they suffer in silence. This is why so many sexual abuse victims often have problems expressing their feelings and feeling a sense of worthiness. For me, this became a pattern I had to spend years unraveling: unlocking my voice, expressing my boundaries, knowing my experiences are valid and deserve to be heard and that I am important.

For so many years later I downplayed my experience out of embarrassment, shrugging it off like it wasn't a big deal, even though I knew it was affecting me in how my body was responding sexually through numbness and pain, *and* how it was affecting my relationships to men. I would experience pleasure and then contract immediately afterwards and push them away. Pleasure equaled shame and was extremely confusing. I had no healthy concept of what boundaries were, because when your physical and sexual boundaries get crossed so young it is extremely difficult to even know what a boundary is as a result.

That first sexual experience being one of confusion, and violation of my physical and sexual boundaries created a deep imprint in my psyche. But this original wound has become my greatest gift on my own healing journey and through all the work I have done with women over the past decade in healing their own relationships to their bodies, sexuality and the masculine. I was able to alchemize the trauma into my greatest source of power. I believe we are not victims of the things that happen to us, nor do we attract them to ourselves, as some spiritual beliefs teach that "everything is your mirror" and "you create your own reality." Try saying that to anyone who has suffered some traumatic abuse that they attracted and created that experience, and watch them punch you square in the face. Telling someone they attract everything to them when it comes to trauma is a classic form of spiritual bypassing and it has to stop because, no, we do not attract horrific things to ourselves. I believe we are born into these fleshy bodies with a soul curriculum that is pre-written in the stars before we incarnate, and we can never fully understand the *why* of all these things that occur along our soul's journey. It is simply a mystery, and no one deserves horrible things to happen to them. But for whatever reason these things happen and it is part of the grand mystery of life. The important thing is that we take responsibility by calling back our power to ourselves, we learn the soul lessons, we alchemise the pain and we choose not to remain a victim to our stories or let them define us. This is when we find true power.

Experiencing abuse of any kind in the first seven years of life changes you forever. Many traditional societies saw a divine order in life, including the idea that every stage of life offers a specific set of challenges and lessons that add to our maturity and support our individuation. In the early 20th century, Rudolf Steiner, the great seer and philosopher, offered his own map of life that revealed some of the important lessons we must master as we develop. Steiner presented this map as 10 seven-year cycles that all of us who make it to the age of 70 years old must pass through. If we confront the lessons of each cycle with courage, honesty, and sincerity, the lessons will be mastered and our psychological and spiritual development will bring forth great rewards. According to his model, infancy to age seven is the stage of growing down and fully landing into the physical dimension from the spiritual dimension. It is also about differentiating from the biological mother. These years are very formative and it is when our seven chakras are being formed. What happens psychologically in these first seven years is where all our early imprints and conditionings begin, determining how we view the world and if we deem it to be a safe place as well as every other major belief system. Many people, like myself, experience sexual abuse during this first seven year cycle, and this is what marks their primary imprints and conditioning around sex, the body, and safety. The next seven years, seven to 14, are the years preparing for puberty and coming of age. This is a very powerful initiation period in which a rebirth takes place, marked by hormonal changes that move us into puberty. We have landed and are now incarnating as a sexual being.

It was at the end of my second seven year cycle, at the age of 14, that another incident occurred which changed me forever—a mystical experience ignited by the original trauma seven years before.

Nadine Lee

A Mystical Experience

A soul-shaking experience that happened when I was 14 ended up helping me define my purpose on this planet, and gave me insight into the driving forces behind my journey of the past two decades to get to where I am now.

It was the summer holidays. I loved spending these warm, sunny days having sleepovers at my girlfriend's house, staying up all night chatting away and doing the usual teenage things. One night I was at my friend's house waiting for my mum to come pick me up, standing in the kitchen sipping on my hot chocolate. I got to chatting with my friend's older brother, who was asking me questions about school and my plans for next year. Then right there, out of nowhere in my friend's family kitchen, I suddenly felt this intense energy rushing through my body. I started to feel what it feels like when you take psychedelics and start leaving the body and blasting off. And yet I had consumed nothing. Intense anxiety began flooding through me as I had no idea what was going on and my nervous system started setting off alarm bells. By the time my mum arrived to pick me up, I was not in a good space. I felt like I had smoked a heap of weed and was totally baked. I was so out of it and incoherent as I attempted to explain what was going on and asked my mom to take me to my grandparents house.

When we arrived at my grandparent's house, I ran straight upstairs to the spare bed and hid under the covers, as if I was on a really bad trip and just needed to wait it out. I barely remember anything from the three-day period I spent at my grandparent's house while I was in this state, but I do remember that the only way I could describe how I felt was "stoned," except I felt like this for three days straight. My mind went completely blank. I had no thoughts running through my head at all. Of course, I now know that the entire goal of meditation and spiritual practices is precisely *to lose the mind*. But to actually be in this state of mindlessness for three days as a 14-year-old girl, with no awareness of what was happening, was frightening. When I looked into the mirror, I had to remind myself of my name, how old I was and where I was. To say that this was terrifying is an understatement. I recall spending most of the time in bed, just hoping I would return to normal. It was like a really bad trip and I had no idea if it was going to end. The one thing I do remember was that every time I was about to go to sleep, I would say to my grandmother and mum, *I think I am going to die tonight in my sleep, so goodbye just in case*. I was convinced I was dying. Little did I know that my physical body wasn't dying, but what I was experiencing was a full blown ego death, a dissolution of self, right there in my grandparent's spare bedroom.

By the fourth day, I woke up and I had thoughts running through my head again. I knew my name, I knew where I was, I knew what school I went to, I felt I could grasp onto some core parts of my identity again. I was indescribably relieved that I didn't completely lose my marbles. However, as with any transcendental experience, you never come back the same. I perceived the world after this experience with a different set of eyes. It was much like after a psychedelic experience, as the third eye which sees beyond the dualistic perception of reality begins to open and therefore wash your two eyes clean of any ignorance. Everything looked different, everything was so clear and it felt like life was breathing through me. But this wasn't some blissful post-psychedelic awakening. First off, there were no psychedelics or substances involved in this experience at all, so it was a real mystery what the heck was going on. At the time I had no awareness of kundalini, spiritual awakenings, trauma, or any spiritual concepts at all for that matter. I recall sitting out behind our family home staring at the trees and asking my mum those same questions I asked as a six year old: *Who am I? What is the purpose of all this? Why am I here? Is this real?* But this time, it wasn't laced with a light-hearted curiosity, it was laced with intense terror and genuinely needing to know the answer to these questions in order to make sense of what the heck just happened to me and how I could just move on with my life and get back to who I was before this all went down. My mum had no idea how to answer my questions.

I felt alone, scared, and like I was downright losing it. These intense questions riddled me for many more months and I found no answers. This was a time where the Internet was just beginning and social media did not exist, so my options of seeking information were limited to my local library, where I found nothing of substance. I was hesitant to share what was going on in my inner world with anyone, because I was legitimately worried that I would be locked up in a mental asylum. This is when things started getting even weirder. My perception of reality was so fragmented from this experience that I started to question everything and experience frightening delusions and paranoias. I was not sure what was real, and I started asking questions like, *What if I am dead and I am a ghost? What if I am in a Truman show? What if all these people and everything is a figment of my imagination?* It started getting scary when I started thinking that people were trying to poison me with some substance that would make me go back into that state I was in for those mystical and mysterious three days. By this time I was convinced I had lost it, but stillI kept it all very quiet so nobody would know what was going on inside of me. I tried to cope by filling my mind with lots of thoughts, ensuring that I would never go back into a "mindless" state. This felt the safest coping mechanism, and so I started to become fixated on my school work, overcompensating with intellect. Complex mathematical problems, physics and economics became my obsession. Naturally, my school work flourished and I was getting top grades because I was obsessed with keeping my mind busy. The other way I coped with this inner turmoil was by creating art. Painting had always been healing for me, but my art began taking a psychedelic turn. I started painting lots of flowers, and womb/vagina-like images with vibrations around them. When I was in my mid-20s and discovered the work of Alex Grey, the great visionary artist of our time, it was a major aha moment when I realized that my artwork was visionary—which is what artists paint after they have psychedelic experiences. This art is a way to speak the unspoken from the transcendent experience. Here I was, a 14-year-old girl who had a mysterious mystical experience, and was now painting psychedelic flowers and female genitalia. I believe that through the art, my higher self was speaking to me, guiding me on what I had to do in order to integrate this experience—namely, connect with nature, my body, and sexuality; the feminine.

The problem was, I felt safe and in control when I lived in my mind, so this is where I lived for most of my teenage years. But I was suffering in silence. The paranoia got worse, along with spells of intense social anxiety. I started to self-harm and starve myself as further ways to gain a sense of control over my reality. This lasted until my late teens when I reached a rock bottom and begged my mother to take me to see a psychiatrist. One of the worst memories I have was calling my best friend in the middle of the night because I had cut my arms with my scissors in one of my darkest depressive episodes. Another memory was being on our end of school break during the peak of my anorexia. I was so strict with my diet regime and my weight that after every night out I would make sure I woke up at 6am and went for a 10km run to burn off the one glass of wine I had the night before. I was miserable.

When I finally saw the psychiatrist, they diagnosed me with a whole heap of 'disorders' and prescribed the usual antidepressant medication. At this point I was so desperate that I took the pills, although I only lasted a couple of months on them. I didn't know what was worse, being numb on these pills, suffering even more anxiety and full-body shaking tremors every day or being the way I was without the pills. I knew I needed to find some kind of alternative support. When I did some research on antidepressants and saw that "suicidal tendencies" is a "common" side effect, I knew I needed to get off this medication. I knew why my mother had tried to prevent me from taking them for so long. Even though she felt helpless not knowing what was going on with me, she herself had limited resources. By chance (or more likely, divine intervention), I was walking out of the psychiatrist's office one day, vowing to never go back, when I saw a poster for a meditation and yoga class. Desperate, I took myself to this class full of hippies, where dreadlocks were the look and the smell of nag champa incense and patchouli stenched in everyone's clothes. I surrendered to the guidance. The teacher started guiding us into stillness, closing our eyes and focusing our concentrated awareness on a mantra *so-hum*, inhale *so*, exhale *hum*. I had no idea what this meant, but I did the thing and something so profound happened... Finally I felt calm, finally I felt anxiety-free and thought-free, but without the paranoia that I would lose my mind again. I finally felt back to myself again. From this moment forward my life and healing journey took a 180, from medication to meditation. Everything I once judged ("the hippies") I was on the path to becoming. This path was working for me and I was finally getting answers.

How do I explain what happened to me? If you look at the nature of trauma, you could say my experience was a prolonged trauma response—specifically, the flight response, for I completely left my body for three days straight. This is one lens to perceive this experience and a valid one that I feel holds some truth, especially because it was triggered by talking to an older boy, my friend's brother, who reminded me of my abuser. The other is the mystical lens, whereby I had experienced a full-blown spontaneous kundalini awakening, and massive shift in consciousness as a result. This is why spiritual teachers like Gopi Krishna say there is a razor's edge between the mystic and the madman; the line is very thin. In fact, there are reports of shamans going into mental asylums and all they see is humans whose spiritual or energy bodies are disassociated from their physical bodies, which is usually a result of trauma. Trauma causes us to leave the body and *disassociate*, which is a mechanism designed to protect us from having a psychotic break, because the emotions associated with that traumatic event are too intense to face, especially as a young child. However, if we do get faced with the traumatic event again, we can actually experience a "psychotic break," which I believe is, from my own experience, consciousness leaving the body— which also feels like a mystical awakening. The psychiatry world has barely any understanding of what is happening from the spiritual perspective and therefore I believe a big part of my life's work is to offer from my own direct experience an alternative pathway to understanding mental health and healing. It was very clear that since my consciousness left the body completely, through the spiritual visions and messages I was getting I was to now learn how to *inhabit my body fully* and feel safe in my body fully. For this, I had to begin my journey into the underworld, which is where I met my first shadow teacher, who played a pivotal role in helping me to revisit that original sexual trauma—this time in a conscious way— and liberate myself from its shackles and the power it was holding over me.

The Shadow Teacher Appears

I believe with my whole being that when the student is ready, the teachers appear. In the case of the meditation class, I was beyond ready. I was desperate, begging on my knees for support. I also believe that we have to get to this breaking point, rock bottom or full-blown breakdown, in order for the breakthrough to come. After this one meditation class, I was committed to learning more, and the obsession with self-healing began. The teachers were appearing effortlessly as I was so receptive and ready. I never had to seek out any teachers and I was so blessed to have lived with some powerful beings, literally living with all sorts of teachers including shamans, advaita vedanta masters, tantrika women, and iyengar yoga masters. I believe it was because I had zero attachment to 'getting anything' from them, in terms of becoming a spiritual teacher or teaching their work that they were so open and receptive to me. I simply wanted to heal myself. That was my main focus. I wanted to understand what happened to me when I was seven and 14 years old, and how I could repair my fragmented psyche.

I knew I needed to begin this descent into the body to face the original trauma and the associated emotions. Tantra was always something that interested me, and I knew it held a key for me to begin this descent. It was when I met my first Tantra teacher that my healing truly started to integrate and so did my life's purpose. I was living in Sydney at the time and my best friend had a "tantra teacher" male friend who she used to get yoni massages from. She suggested I book a "yoni massage" session with this guy, thinking it might help me heal the wounds of my sexual trauma. I was a little weary of the whole thing, but I was open to anything at this point as my devotion to self-healing and realization had become the most important thing in my life.

It was one of those synchronistic meetings that was always destined to happen. Soon after my friend suggested the yoni massage, I went away for the weekend with a friend north of Sydney and happened to meet a couple who owned the house that this tantric healer was subletting in Sydney for the week, offering his yoni massage sessions. I saw this as a powerful and extremely synchronistic sign from the universe that I had to meet this man.

As it turned out, he was one of a kind and one of the key teachers, healers, and initiates on my path. He was a typical Scorpio—intense, deep, no bullshit. The Scorpionic energy was just what I was needing to support the illumination of my own shadows and explore the hidden parts of myself. This is why I call him one of my shadow teachers. He was sent to me to support me exploring all the parts of myself I had repressed and that lay dormant in the unconscious, the shadows of my psyche. I ended up booking a session with him and showing up so nervous. The session was not what I expected. We just talked in the healing room about my sexuality, what happened to me as a child, my relationship with my father and men in general, and then we just did some breathing practices. There was no yoni massage at all. I actually wanted to become friends with him because I am always a sucker for Scorpios (they can meet my Cancerian depths). I had a strong sense that this man was going to teach me a lot. We developed a friendship and later I moved back to Brisbane, where he was based. After connecting a few times as friends, we eventually became lovers. He was 20 years older than me and we got the most judgemental stares whenever we were out in public, but I didn't care. I knew I was healing some father/masculine wounds and I thought it was a great opportunity to heal in an embodied, experiential workshop: aka, a relationship dojo. We had this relationship for about a year while I was studying nutrition and offering catering services to retreats, and he was leading sexual healing retreats. Naturally, he asked me to cater the food for them. I loved offering the nourishment for these deep transformational retreats, yet I had zero desire to participate in whatever he was teaching. In fact, I thought what he was doing was a bit strange. I would walk by the room and see the glimpses of the groups he was leading doing all sorts of emotional release practices and sexual practices: yelling, screaming, orgasm-ing, just going wild and completely unhinged. Out of context these types of practices can look very odd from the outsider glancing in.

At the time, I had never seen a human expression like this, completely sober (drunk or on drugs, yes). So whenever he would ask me to sit in on the sessions I refused and said, "I am not into whatever you guys are doing, I will just stick to the food part." I had zero attachment to learning what he taught, but because we were lovers, my body received so many codes, information and healing from him. Because he offered sexual healings for women as a profession, I was getting the VIP treatment, and many of our sexual interactions were deep and profound healing sessions for me. He helped me explore the deepest aspects of my psyche through our sexual connection. He helped me find my "no," find my voice, and own my power—by taking me to my depths, deeper than I could have ever taken myself.

One day we were walking through the forest at sunset, and a memory flashed back of being isolated with an older man when I was seven years old. I felt so unsafe, and my body started reacting, heart beating, sweating, fear filling my being. We were the only ones in the forest at sunset, and we actually ended up getting lost in the dark, unsure how to get back to the car. Meanwhile, flashbacks of being confined with an older man were coming to the forefront of my awareness, and that original trauma in my body resurfaced. I recall some very irrational fears arising that he was going to harm me. However, as I dropped out of my mind and the irrational fears arising, and into my body, I knew I was not in any real danger.

Another incident was exploring a surrender play, whereby he tied me up to the bed and blindfolded me and would introduce different sensations to my body—a feather, the smell of an essential oil, a flower over my body. This was such a powerful practice of facing the fear of the unknown, and rebuilding that trust in the masculine that was lost from my original sexual abuse. This was a very powerful practice that again brought up a lot of irrational fears: *What if he hurts me? What if he takes advantage of me? I am completely unable to move and I have a blindfold on.* But because of the safe space that was created (we agreed he would stop at any point I wanted him to), this process allowed me to surrender, yet also feel in control at the same time.

These were both examples of powerful experiences in recalling soul fragments. This is what happens when we as adults consciously relive an original trauma, with greater awareness. As we do this, it allows us to feel the feelings that we couldn't exactly process as the younger version of ourselves who was abused or violated. This is a big part of the work I do now with my clients, supporting them to relive the original trauma and finally feel the feelings they could not feel and express back when the trauma occurred. It is a way to recall lost parts of our soul that fragment when trauma occurs. When these parts of ourselves are fragmented, we are not whole and we are not embodied. This process of soul retrieval is essential to call back all those parts of us that were fragmented in the original incident through allowing oneself to fully feel what needed to be felt, as an adult, when we are ready to do so.

This relationship was one of the major catalysts for my soul's purpose, allowing me to understand my own sexual psyche and explore these shadow aspects of self, truly moving from victim to victor. This man was the catalyst for me to heal my own sexual trauma and ultimately to offer a space for other women to heal their sexuality.

This man was also a shadow teacher in the sense that I saw a lot of backlash to his work with the wider community of women, whom many felt he violated their personal boundaries in sessions. This is unfortunately very common among male tantric practitioners, and as much as I believed in his work, I knew there was still a lot of work he needed to do around his *own* shadow sexual motives to prevent these women from feeling that they were getting re-traumatised. Sexual trauma is such a fragile thing to work with. Inadvertently, he ended up being the inspiration for me to create the core foundation of healing women's sexuality through learning to feel safe—for women to take power back in their own hands and begin this journey on their own with the guidance and support of another woman. Through my experience with having this man as a close ally and lover, I started to move from the safety of my head and began to descend into my body. The judgment I held around this work was because my soul knew this was the work I was soon to be called to, but my ego was resisting in every possible way. It is funny how this happens. Our souls magnetize to us the exact experiences we need, the perfect teachers we need, but our minds try to resist the path at all cost and stick to what is safe and known. It was when I truly just let go and surrendered to this path that everything began to unfold.

Becoming Embodied

Working with my sexuality on a somatic embodied level with this partner was the missing link all along. It is what I needed to ground the spiritual energy that blasted me open at 14. From what I understand about kundalini energy, it is our life force energy that lays dormant at the base of our spine. When it rises due to being evoked in spiritual practice, psychedelics, or in my case, spontaneously—which can often be triggered by traumatic memories—it can in fact rise up too quickly and blast someone open. When this happens, the energy gets concentrated in the third eye and crown chakras, and leaves someone very open psychically and spiritually but very ungrounded. In the Western medical world, this is often mistaken for mental illness. I believe this is what happened to me. I wasn't prepared to hold this much spiritual energy; it was like plugging into a high voltage electrical current. I hadn't yet prepared my nervous system or worked through the traumas held in my first two chakras from the original sexual trauma and unresolved emotions that resided in my body as a result. It is so important to prepare oneself for the powerful electricity that is kundalini to open us up to higher states of consciousness. In my case, the energy rose and blasted out. Because of my unresolved traumas, the energy couldn't flow all the way through my body because of the blockages from the unresolved traumas, and it essentially ended up spinning out of control in my third eye, causing paranoia, anxiety, mood swings and delusions. This is why I am so passionate about embodiment work because in the spiritual world where everyone wants to ascend and leave the body, this can be a dangerous thing. This is where the tantric path differs. It is truly about the entire integrated full-spectrum human experience, starting from the root and rising to the crown, embracing everything and denying nothing. It is about merging one's sexuality and spirituality, one's feminine and masculine, in union. Having discovered firsthand the dangers of kundalini rising without proper preparation, my entire mission has been to heal the lower chakras, which are the seat of the feminine, and to develop my roots while practicing yoga as the foundation to heal and prepare the nervous system for kundalini energy to rise safely.

Those sexual, feminine and nature-based visionary art images that I created after my mystical experience were a hint of the healing journey to come. It all made sense when I met my teachers in my 20s and was shown that we are not here to blast out of our bodies, without solid foundations and roots. We are here to have a human embodied experience of our divinity. We came from Source from pure consciousness—that is the familiar part. Our role as a human incarnation is to be a spirit having a *human experience.* And so this is where my focus landed, on the descent into the body. Through this journey of descent I discovered the true power of the feminine, of sacred sexuality, and the ancient archetype of the sex priestess.

This descent is not always pretty, because to truly inhabit our human body, to become truly embodied, means we have to feel all that is uncomfortable in the body. All our suppressed emotions get stored in the body, not in the mind. The mind cannot store energy in motion (emotions) but the cells of our body can, so this is where we must go in order to free up that energy once again. And of course the place where we store the most emotions as women is the second chakra, our womb. This leads me to our first code, *Opening the Womb Portal*, the first step to embodying the sex priestess.

CODE 1:

OPENING THE WOMB PORTAL

The journey to reclaiming our power as women starts and ends—like all things—in the womb.

This first code is a crucial one for every woman to unlock. Opening my womb portal was the foundation of my soul's work in this lifetime and the process of finding my true power by releasing the trapped emotions stored in my body. Earlier in my journey, I remember meeting women in the spiritual communities who would say their womb told them to do this or that, and I had no idea what they were talking about. I would deeply contemplate... *How can your womb tell you something? How can your body even tell you something?* I was living so deep in my head that anything below the throat wasn't a source of information or wisdom; it was just a bodily function. I had learned to stay in the safe container of logic, for keeping myself within the boundaries of my rational mind was what saved me from losing my marbles when I had my kundalini awakening. To dive deep into the depths of my being—to take a descent below my logical brain—felt instinctively terrifying. I was afraid of what I would find there. It felt wild, feral, out of control. I was afraid of the rage I had suppressed from being sexually abused, afraid of the pain of my childhood, of all the emotions I never allowed myself to feel unless I was intoxicated.

No matter how afraid we may be, this journey of descent is one that each of us must summon the courage to take, making our first steps inward to the sacred temple of our bodies—a space which we may have abandoned or neglected for a long time.

Opening the womb portal is the core work of feminine embodiment, for the womb is the portal of creation and the seat of a woman's power. And as it is the portal of creation, it must also be the portal of death, for there is no creation without something dying first. In that death is the darkness, the depth, the pain, the agony; all of those parts of us that have been exiled, that long to be felt. For when we feel, we heal. The feminine is the embodiment of the darkness, for she is the womb—the zero-space or creative void from which all life is birthed. To fear the darkness is to fear the feminine. To deny the body is to deny the feminine. Opening the womb portal is more of a descent into the underworld, into the unconscious, and it is in the body itself where the unconscious repressed emotions are stored. In order to find our true power, we must shine light on all that is keeping us small and trapped: those aspects of our psyche that, if not illuminated, hold immense power over us.

To open the womb portal is the deepest initiation into the feminine that you will ever undertake. From menstruation, to birthing a child, to menopause, to every act of love-making, to every creation that gets birthed through you in your lifetime—it all takes place through the womb portal, the feminine seat of power and wisdom. This is a sacred process that each woman must undertake on her own, feeling her way through the dark, guided by her own instincts and intuition. So many of us on the spiritual path think we must seek the answers in courses and certification programs and healers and gurus, when all along the answers are waiting to be unlocked within our own body (for women specifically, within our womb space).

Initiation into the Womb

The womb is the portal of gnosis (embodied wisdom), and my experience at a tantric ashram in India was my first true initiation into her power, depth and potency.

It was one of those great cosmic jokes that I was led halfway around the world to India, the motherland of tantra, to spend the next few months studying the tantric teachings and practices— only to find myself learning the art of tantra from my own body, not from the gurus and disciplines in the ashram. I had saved up thousands of dollars from the tantric dakini work I had started doing back in Australia to go straight to the ashrams of India, where I thought I would get my 'official' tantric initiation.

I had already answered the call of womb initiation a couple years before by following my deep desire to work with the dark feminine archetype within myself. The work I did to fund this educational and spiritual pilgrimage was the work that called me into meeting my dark seductress feminine—the work of the tantric dakini, which we'll be exploring more in *Code 6: Initiatrix of Awakening*. This was a part of me that longed to be met, yet was shamed by society, and I internally shamed myself on a very deep and subtle level. You can call her Kali, Lilith, the dark goddess—she was the one who had woken up in me. She is the one who dwells in the womb space—the absolute void, the darkest of all darks, the point of conception, the black hole from which everything is birthed. She invites us into the parts of ourselves that are still in the dark, repressed and yearning to be expressed.

It all started with an intense desire to explore my dormant and repressed inner seductress. I was contemplating either becoming a exotic dancer or doing dakini work, offering men tantric embodiment sessions. I chose the second option. It felt natural and effortless to me, as men were constantly asking to "spend time in my shakti energy." I figured, *Yes you can spend time in my shakti energy, but you have to pay me*. So I began creating containers, sacred spaces, for these men to explore their eros, their desire, and to be witnessed in their expression. This work was very intuitive. I felt like I was picking up where I had left off in a previous lifetime as a tantrika. I would guide these men into meditation practices and teach them how to breathe and circulate energy through their body, which naturally led to releasing buried traumas and suppressed emotions in their bodies and healing unresolved mother issues. The exchange was mutually beneficial. I was completely in control, which helped me heal my own feelings of being a "victim" to male sexuality, stemming from the sexual violation I endured as a child. Plus, by doing this work proudly and out in the open, I was clearing lifetimes of shame held around the archetype of the sacred prostitute. To be clear, I was not having sex with any of these men. But sexual energy was very much present, and I consciously used it to evoke their eros, supporting them in channelling it through specific tantric practices.

The deep shame around this once-sacred expression of the feminine had long been present in my darkest shadows. Now, I was exploring this archetype and bringing her to light. I could feel myself stepping into a deeper embodiment of my power through my fully expressed dark eros. This part of the female psyche is so shamed and cast aside into the depths of the unconscious, the part that has been conditioned to fear and deny her sexual power. It holds so much power over so many women through the knots of karmic shame.

I did this work for about 12 months when I felt the call to get some sort of 'official' tantra training. I was still stuck in old programming from the education system I grew up with, telling me that I needed a certificate in order to do what I naturally knew how to do and was good at; to somehow legitimize my capabilities. But sometimes mistakes can be portals to wisdom, and by letting that play out, I ended up realizing that I had the wisdom inside me all along.

Kali, the black one, the goddess of death and rebirth, was my guiding force during this womb portal initiation phase. So when an ex-boyfriend invited me to a tantric ashram in India named after the deity herself, I didn't think twice before booking my one-way ticket to India. My time at the ashram was interesting on many levels. I remember arriving there and, being the hypersensitive creature that I am, immediately felt darkness seeping through the walls and the energetic field of the space. I knew I was in the right place for this dark Goddess initiation, but I had no idea what was about to take place.

Something did not feel right at this place. First off, it was run by white American men. This was a red flag, because everything I had ever read and known in my cells told me that the feminine was the initiator of tantra. And in the three months I lived there, I only ever met the guru once—and he creeped me out in a big way. I've always had a secret obsession with cults, fascinated by their psychology and how they draw people in. Instantly I knew I was in a cult of sorts. I also knew enough to never let myself drink the kool aid.

For the first month I spent there, I lived in a tiny, simple cabin. But this dark force field of energy was all-consuming. I knew I had to get out and find some space for myself while still learning and enjoying the ashram. I've always been this way. I don't like to conform and will find a way to make a situation suit me. As things progressed, I ended up leaving the ashram and finding my own apartment living among the villagers. I wanted the real Indian experience. So what did I do? I got myself a local boyfriend—an Indian guy six years younger than me from the village. It was living there with him and the locals that I got a real education in tantra. I remember telling my new boyfriend about all these texts we were reading and explaining to him some of the teachings inside my books, and he said, "Oh yeah, Shiva, Vishnu, Rama... Yeah I know them, they are all my friends." The teachings were so integrated into his life that he didn't need to arduously chant or study the sutras like I was doing down the road at the ashram. While the philosophy was fascinating, it was taking me out of my body and directly into intellect, which was the opposite of what I had come for. I wanted to learn tantra *in my body*.

Then there were the weekly 'pujas' at the ashram, which were tantric rituals where the men honored the goddess through a series of mantras. The women sat before the man and he would chant, offer us flowers and wreaths, and stare deeply into our eyes in order to enter a transpersonal dimension. They would see the divine feminine through us as we sat channeling the goddess herself. This was a beautiful ritual, but again, it was not embodied. It was clear from what I saw and felt that these men were not truly honoring the feminine. No women were leading any classes, and I felt a distinctly "boys club" energy every time I spoke to any of the male teachers. So I went to my Indian lover in hopes of receiving real embodied goddess worship—which I certainly did. This man was 21 years old, and I remember feeling so safe, seen and honored as the goddess I am every time we would make love and in our everyday interactions. My body was receiving the initiation I needed, the embodied goddess *puja*.

The most powerful teaching I received during my time at the ashram was the deeply embodied initiation into my womb. As part of the curriculum, women were meant to stay in their cabins or in solitude as much as possible when they were bleeding, and were not allowed to attend any classes. Their rationale for keeping the women at home was their belief the women would affect the group energy field because our auric fields are 10 times amplified during menstruation. I knew this was a tradition in Indian culture and that women aren't allowed to enter temples during their menses, so it did make sense. Plus, I didn't mind having some time off from our jam-packed schedule of classes.

During my first solitary bleeding time, I was walking through the isolated forest between the ashram and the coastline, and I had this wild idea to take off my pants and bleed directly into the earth. That moment is when I felt that I fully received the transmission from the ashram. At an ashram named after Kali herself, I felt her potent force of death, rebirth and transformation right between my legs as the blood dripped into the earth. This was such a primal moment and it felt so embodied, liberating and free. Before this I had never actually connected to my blood, using pads and tampons that quickly absorb the blood and being done with it by throwing it in the trash bin. I was so disconnected from this primal and natural aspect of myself, as so many other women are too.

This was what I came to India to learn. This was one of the deepest initiations I received from my time at the ashram, and ironically, it had nothing to do with anyone teaching me any specific philosophy or practice. My body was simply teaching me everything I needed to know. As each month went by, I would go deeper into this blood ritual, noticing how much more embodied I felt in my feminine power. I loved connecting to the smell of it and observing the energetic texture each month. It was teaching me so much about my body and what was going on inside of me.

A Shamanic Death and Rebirth

The veil is so thin between the subconscious and conscious mind when a woman bleeds. Every month as I consciously went into this shamanic death and rebirth ceremony happening inside of my body, I got to pierce the veil of my own consciousness and see what was lying dormant in my own subconscious mind. It was an opportunity to feel it fully through and thus alchemize it from my body. At that time in my life, a lot of emotions, memories and energies would arise around being prosecuted or exiled for speaking my truth, and simply for sharing my healing gifts with the world. Each month, I went deeper into feeling the pain around these past life memories, along with collective unconscious memories of the female psyche. I cleared them by bringing them to the light of awareness and using embodiment practices to release them from my body, making way for me to stand strong in my truth and share my gifts freely with the world without fear of prosecution. As this practice developed my own exploration of my womb and the power that dwells there, I began teaching other women to do the same. A body of work called Menstruation Magic was born, first as an eBook and then a live workshop I taught around the world, including Dubai, Bali, London, New York City, and all over Australia.

To fear menstrual blood is to fear our feminine essence. The blood is literally our feminine sacred elixir and connects us to the deepest core of our power, to the power of creation, our womb. It is the physical lining of the uterus womb space that holds all the nutrients and energetic power to house a human being to grow every single month. The blood that sheds every month is a symbol of death and rebirth, the end of one cycle and the beginning of another. For there cannot be death without creation and rebirth. I believe that the process of death and rebirth itself is the truest embodiment of the feminine, so to deny or be disconnected to the literal elixir that represents that is to be disconnected to the feminine itself. Whenever I work with women in unlocking their sex priestess codes, I always start with womb work and their relationship to their menstruation.

The womb is a bridge between the worlds, a portal of creation that literally births human life. How fascinating is that—a speck of stardust is conceived by the universe and makes its way to the earth via a woman's womb portal. This is the power and force the female body holds. Woman is the true shaman, the bridge between the seen and unseen worlds. Every month that we go through the menstruation process, we are also experiencing a shamanic death and rebirth. This happens when we shed the lining of the uterus, when conception of a child does not occur. During this process of the uterus lining shedding and exiting the body through the blood, so too does anything that is being held deep in a woman's subconscious mind—anything below or beyond the light of her conscious awareness—as the womb is the gateway to the subconscious. Every month that she bleeds, she gets an opportunity to face what she has absorbed in terms of the emotional energy within and around her, if she chooses to do so.

The womb is the darkest place in a woman's body. As the source of a woman's power of creation, it is symbolized by the darkness itself, the void, as the portal to creation. The womb is a black hole that light and life is conceived from. We truly can understand that from darkness, light is born, from the void all creation is birthed. This is what is literally happening inside of a woman's body. She holds these embodied codes within her by simply having a womb space.

Like the black holes in the universe that absorb energy towards them, so too does the womb. Like the feminine as a whole, it is magnetic. As a microcosm of the macrocosm, the womb absorbs a lot of energy, and often not the best kind. Because the womb has this self-cleansing mechanism every month, it can act somewhat like a filtration system for a woman's emotional body, absorbing all and any emotions that are not processed in her emotional body every month. The body naturally releases this emotional energy each month through the blood.

However, if a woman is not connecting to her menstrual cycle consciously, then she is going to experience what Western science terms "premenstrual syndrome," which includes everything from headaches to intense cramps, high levels of blood loss, blood clots, pain and mood swings. In my experience working with thousands of women and in my own explorations over the past decade working consciously with my menstrual cycle, I can assure you that the discomfort we experience before we bleed is not a syndrome at all. In fact, it is a blessing. This may not seem like a blessing if you are a woman experiencing a lot of pain and discomfort before and during your cycle, but hear me out. Your physical pain is an indication that there is emotional pain that must be addressed. Your body is inviting you into an unconscious negative emotion that may have been buried very deep down inside you for way too long—some emotion that has been swept into the basement of your subconscious and not acknowledged.

As you probably already know, when we suppress any emotion, it doesn't go away; instead, it gets stuck in some corner of the body. This is the cause of most physical illnesses. It almost always roots back to emotional sickness. As women, we have this magical opportunity every month to be shown exactly what wants to be retrieved from the attic of our subconscious, through our body signaling to us with physical and emotional contractions. When the veil between the conscious mind and subconscious mind gets very thin just before we bleed, these suppressed emotions have their chance to finally get our attention. If we choose to listen and feel what's there, it actually invites us deeper into the body to tune into ourselves and ask what is the message and what does the body need, allowing the emotion and thereby the physical pain to be alchemised. Honestly, it is as simple as that. It's just about creating space to feel what's beneath the physical pain.

I like to use the analogy of the monster in that attic that just wants to be seen and accepted, but the more we shove him back into that hidden attic to be ignored, the bigger and more mean and angry he gets, until he starts trying to get attention by wreaking havoc on our lives. The more you ignore your emotions, the more intense they get every month in the manifestation of period pain. And remember that your womb is your portal of creation. If you are in a muddled unconscious place that is blocked by a backlog of unprocessed emotions, that is where you are creating from. As Carl Jung said, "Until you make the unconscious conscious, it will direct your life and you will call it fate." The work is to bring consciousness to the unconscious. Every emotion, and every part of ourselves that the emotion represents, just wants to be felt, seen, loved and accepted. Doing this helps them to be liberated and released.

Before I knew how to alchemise my emotions, I had heavy periods and a lot of cramping. I would ignore these bodily signals that were inviting me to look at a deeper emotion; and as a result, the pain would amplify with every passing month. What we resist really does persist. Our wombs are literally speaking to us every single month, inviting us into our repressed unconscious emotions as a gateway to free us—an opportunity to be reborn free from the shackles of old stored memories that literally want to be bled out of us every 28 or so days. When I started implementing the emotional alchemy practices that I'll share at the end of the chapter, I started to feel my emotions to their depths, and it would create so much spaciousness in my body, so much lightness. The physical pain, whether it was premenstrual cramping, or any other pain in my body indicating that an emotion wanted to be felt, would literally dissipate within minutes. Now, I literally bleed for one day, with zero period pain at all. If I do have the odd contraction, I will drop straight into the feeling using the Emotional Alchemy technique I'll be teaching you, and it will be alchemised very quickly.

Here's the really important thing to remember with all of this: the feminine is the darkness, it is what creates depth within us, it is the substance. And as a woman becomes more embodied in her depth, she learns to embrace pain, embrace death, embrace transformation—all through her monthly cycle. If she truly wants to embrace and embody the light fully, she must first anchor in the feminine darkness, the death that makes way for rebirth, which is the essence of female power. This is the first initiation into our womanhood and into our power as the creators that we are. It's not about ascending to the light; we start by descending into the darkest depths and rooting there. Our period is in no way at all a monthly burden. It is an invitation each month to die and be reborn. The shamanic principles that are spoken of intellectually are literally happening inside a woman's body. To understand and truly embody the power of women, womb-bearing beings, as the creators—this is the feminine in her fullest expression.

This is the first code of the sex priestess because it is where she gets the opportunity to be self-initiated through her own body. She learns from the darkness, she rebirths from her own womb into the light of who she truly is. She finds her depths and substance and strong roots into the earth that anchor her fully into this earth plane, so that she can move energy through her body and explore the higher dimensions without losing her groundedness. The priestess has to have a foot in both worlds. She must learn to master both the light and the dark. She is not just living in the light, she also needs to know how to hold her power in the dark. The womb portal is the self-initiation and embodiment of this principle. Every month, you are invited to shine the light of awareness on all that has been cast into the shadows of your psyche, waiting to be alchemised. When you have the ability to do this for yourself, then you can truly do this for others as the healing priestess you are.

And it's not just for you; it's also in service of your beloved. The Sex Priestess is activated when she makes love to her man, and through her womb portal, she has the ability to absorb his unconscious and support him in alchemising all that is unseen, giving him the opportunity to rebirth himself into his truest self. She has the power to free him from all shackles of the unconscious conditionings and programs that hold him back from his own liberation.

Opening the Womb Portal: Core Practices

Consciously Menstruating

The Menstruation phase is the bleeding phase of your cycle, days one to five, roughly. First, you want to allow one to two days of solitude, ideally the first two days of your period. This is your time to connect to yourself, reflect, allow the emotions to flow through, and give yourself space to die and be reborn. It is also when your energetic field is the largest and your yin energy is at its peak, so you are extremely receptive to receiving information from your higher self—make sure you create space and silence for this. I always turn off my phone, disconnecting from all technology, social media and external distractions. I spend this time in what I call my 'womb cave' for a minimum of 24 hours, but usually a full 48 hours. This is a time to take yourself on a mini retreat, meditate, sleep, engage in whatever self-care rituals you enjoy, reflect and journal, and blood rituals (more on this in a moment).

The next step is to ditch the pads and tampons and invest in a menstrual cup or period panties. You want to be able to connect to your menstrual blood, so use whatever option is available and most comfortable to you. I love Thinx period panties, which absorb your blood so that you have the chance to rinse out the panties and capture the blood. You can then connect with the blood and offer it back to the earth. However, I find that the menstrual cup is the best option, as you can capture it directly and get to really connect with the color, smell, texture and energy of the blood. As you collect your blood, create a ritual for yourself of offering it back to the earth, as you do this, visualize anything you desire to release back into the earth to be transmuted. You can also visualize your blood acting as an energetic umbilical cord plugging you into the earth's womb.

This helps you feel grounded in your body and plugged into the abundant fertile energy of mother earth.

You might consider using the following journal prompts to help you go deeper into your conscious menstruation phase:

- How am I feeling physically?
- How am I feeling emotionally?
- How am I feeling energetically?
- What wants to be birthed through me this month?
- What am I letting go of this month?
- What are my dreams telling me?
- Where do I desire to invest my energy this month?
- What are my deepest desires to embody and experience this month?
- What are my cramps telling me?
- What is the color and energy of my blood?

Premenstrual phase

The premenstrual phase is the week before you bleed, so days 21-28 of your cycle. The most important thing during this phase is creating space to feel. If you notice you are feeling irritable, heavy, "off" or like things are not flowing, this is usually an indication you are out of alignment because something needs to be addressed within you. Take the time now to observe your emotions so that you can address them. During this phase, be very mindful of what is coming up for you. You want to create space to feel. Journaling is a great place to begin, and then it's important to let the emotions you are feeling be expressed.

Body Awareness

A great practice I guide my clients through is a body awareness practice, starting by simply scanning the body on the physical level first and feeling what is present. Wherever you feel any contractions, or tension, is what you are going to work with. Then it's about acknowledging that sensation by building a mind-body connection. For example, *I am feeling tension in my lower belly*. Start to breathe into that part of your body and give it some sound and movement. Once you feel complete, then it's time to go deeper. Beneath the physical is the emotional. What emotions are arising? Breath into the emotion and allow yourself to feel it fully. Validate the emotions by stating out loud, *I am feeling shame in my lower belly*. Then you want to give that emotion an expression. How does shame sound? What posture does shame take in your body? You want to give the emotion a full range of expression in order to move it through and out of your entire physical and emotional body.

The more you do this every time strong emotions arise, especially in your premenstrual phase, the lighter your periods will be and the less cramps you will experience, because you are addressing and alchemising the emotions before they start to build up and create more tension through cramps and emotional turmoil within you.

Emotional Alchemy

The next phase is the Emotional Alchemy practice, which involves expanding upon what came up in the body awareness practice and amplifying the most prominent emotion in order to release it. The key to emotional alchemy is giving the emotion that is arising its fullest expression so that it can be seen, felt and subsequently released from your physical body. It is not enough to just journal about your feelings and try to replace them with positive affirmations. This work is much deeper, more embodied, and truly effective at getting to the root emotion causing you physical pain. Below are some ways to release common emotions effectively, or what I refer to as "Emotional Alchemy." Once you feel and express the emotions through, you alchemise them into higher states of consciousness through creating space in your body.

Fear & Somatic Shaking

All animals do this when faced with fear. After a gazelle is chased by a tiger and almost killed, its sympathetic nervous system is activated as it is riddled with fear of almost being eaten alive, and the gazelle will shake its body for a period of time to reset the nervous system. What the gazelle is doing is effectively releasing the fear from its body and nervous system so that it can return to a neutral baseline state. This is a very simple practice that you can do if fear is arising. Put on a powerful bass or shamanic drumming track for a minimum of 10 minutes and shake your body. Focus on grounding your feet deeply rooted in the earth and feel your hips relaxed, your genitals relaxed, your jaw relaxed, your hips fluid and shake like a wild woman. Shake it all out and imagine you are releasing any fear from your very cells as you do this. Make sure your hips are fluid, not stiff, as this is where a lot of fear gets stored.

Shame & Twerking

Yep, you heard me: twerking. Think about the stigma around twerking: you might have an instant reaction that this is "something nasty hoes do." I invite you to feel that shame and let it go by facing that nasty hoe inside of you who is totally shame-free and just waiting to be unleashed. But seriously, twerking is an ancient practice used in tribal rituals as a way to collectively release any stuck energy in the root and sacral chakras. And what are the two main emotions that block the root and sacral? Fear and shame. Twerking is such a powerful practice to twerk out any residual shame in your pelvic bowl. When we are menstruating in particular, this amplifies the area of the sacral and a lot of pain can be linked to repressed shame, so twerking can really help release this from the body.

If you need a little inspiration, search for the origins of twerking on YouTube. You'll find tons of videos where you can see powerful African women in tribes together twerking. This practice was a way for the women to bond together as a tribe of sisters. It also helped release stuck energy and acted as a mating call of sorts. It is very primal. I actually remember speaking to a Caribbean woman in Costa Rica about twerking and why women like her all have such amazing butts and twerking abilities. She said it's because they are more connected to the earth, and that this is reflected in their bodies. The booty is literally the symbol of our connection to the earth and our root chakra. By shaking a big booty, it shows we are ready and ripe for pro-creation. As I said, it is a deeply primal aspect of our feminine. To shame the twerking booty is deeply shaming our most primal core feminine. So release the shame and get twerking!

Anger & Pillow Beating

A lot of people (especially women) don't want to admit that they have suppressed anger. If you insist that you're "not an angry person," this practice is probably the one you need most. I always say to my students the one who says they don't have any anger, usually ends up being the one with the most anger in the room. This emotion is incredibly powerful and feared. In terms of frequency, anger isn't actually all that low on the vibrational frequency of emotions; it's actually in the mid-range (shame is the lowest frequency, if you were wondering). When alchemized through healthy expression, anger is what gives us our will power, our willingness to fight for truth and our ability to stand up for ourselves and the things that matter to us. Alchemized anger is pure passion.

The most powerful way to get in touch with your anger, I've found, is to unleash it on a pillow. Activating music helps this process, so find a song that is energizing, with lots of drum and bass. Set up a pillow in front of you and start to move your body, by shaking at first, and then breathing up from the base of your root chakra into your solar plexus. Draw the energy into your hands and start to channel the anger out of your hands and into the pillow. You can start slowly beating the pillow, and then once you get the hang of it just unleash. You can also scream into the pillow! Screaming is so therapeutic—it opens up your throat and sacral chakras, releasing any anger from these places where you have been violated and haven't been able to express your "no." This practice was one of the most powerful for me in accessing my "no" finally after sexual abuse. It is also great for the 'good girl' who is always people-pleasing and has a tendency to be a doormat, letting others walk all over her. If that's you, this practice is your medicine!

Sadness & Somatic Opening

Anger is often the surface-level emotion that covers up deeper feelings of sadness. There can be a deep sadness accumulated from all those times we've allowed ourselves to be walked all over and have our boundaries crossed, betraying ourselves in the process. It's important to feel the anger first and then allow yourself to drop into the sadness underneath. The obvious and most effective way to really feel sadness is crying—and

I mean crying until you feel like your heart is about to break open. Because that is essentially what is happening. The sadness and grief is stored mostly in our heart space, and as we feel the emotion, it breaks open our heart—which has a tendency to become closed off from pain, loss and betrayal—so that more love can flow in and out. Notice if your natural response is to hold back when tears come on, wiping your eyes and trying to block the floodgates. My invitation is to let the floodgates open so that a river of tears can flow. You want to be lying down on your back on a yoga mat, maybe have a pillow next to you to hold or a plush toy to hold onto as your tears flow. Throughout this process, let your body roll around intuitively. The key is to try and stay open, even though it's painful. Keep breathing and opening to the feelings and sensations, even if it literally hurts.

Self-inquiry journaling

In addition to the Emotional Alchemy practices, below are some powerful journaling prompts you can also implement in your next premenstrual phase. However, please use these as the support to the Emotional Alchemy practice, because, like I said, emotions are not going to go away just by journaling about them. Journaling is great for bringing awareness to what is going on, but to truly release the emotions, we have to get into the body and move them through.

- What were the physical sensations you experienced before and during your most recent menstruation?
- What were the emotional themes that arose during your last premenstrual & bleeding phase of your cycle?
- What were the main emotions you experienced?

- When was the first time you ever experienced these emotions?
- What are you holding onto in your life that is no longer serving you?
- What would your life look like if you were to let go of that relationship / career / thought pattern?
- Are there any previous partners that show up strongly in my premenstrual phase? If so, what else do I need to do to let them go?
- What is the hook that keeps me thinking about them?
- In order to truly step into my power, what needs to die within me?

Every month we get invited into the body, into the source of our unconscious. If we choose to accept this invitation, by "going there," we become the true alchemists we are. Again, shamanic death and rebirth isn't just a sexy concept for a woman. Every month she literally has the opportunity to die to the old, and shed out all that no longer serves her from her uterus lining. She sheds the blood, and all the energetic and emotional holding that gets stored in her womb as the seat of the unconscious. When consciously done, she truly takes the time to feel beneath the physical "contractions"—which is her body's way to highlight what wants to be felt in order to be cleared. Her womb then becomes a clearer birthing portal for all that she desires to create through her, from babies to every creation she longs to birth through her creative portal.

One of the deepest core wounds for women is around the masculine, and this will often become prevalent at time of menstruation and premenstruation. It's important not to avoid this but instead to see it as an opportunity to heal. This is especially true if a woman has endured sexual abuse. All these old emotions will arise as they often get buried so deep down in the subconscious and lodged so deeply in the womb itself in the form of shame, fear and grief. With a strong grounding in our own bodies and connection to the embodied power of the womb, we're ready to move onto our next code, where we'll look at healing the relationship to the masculine, both inner and outer, as a core aspect of our Sex Priestess curriculum.

CODE 2:
THE DIVINE MASCULINE

It's true we are living in a man's world. For the past couple thousand years, we have been living in a society built on masculine principles. Is there necessarily anything wrong with this? The masculine is the builder, the doer, the executor of plans and the materializer of the creative visions of the feminine. Where I feel we have gone wrong is that we've focused solely on the masculine while disregarding feminine principles. We are at a point now where we are longing to find more harmony and balance within our society, and this starts by finding harmony within ourselves.

It's not just about bringing back the feminine. We need both sexes working together. We must heal the parts of our inner masculine that are rooted in unhealthy masculine principles. We all have this within us. I heard a quote recently, "Men control the world, but women control the men." I interpret this as a woman and man working harmoniously together, in union. Where the woman will bring forth a creative idea, the man will execute that into the world. It happens by both honoring and listening to one another.

In the second code, we are going to dive deep into integrating and healing your relationship to the masculine. A sex priestess— an empowered integrated woman—must have a healthy relationship to the masculine, as it is expressed in both the men in her life and her own inner masculine. If she wants to be in union with herself and in healthy partnership, this work is essential. With this code, we are going to unveil and alchemize any residual unconscious wounding that might be still lingering from your relationship with your father (your introduction to the masculine and template for relating to the masculine), and then also from every significant male imprint throughout your life. In order to come to a healthy relationship with the masculine in our lives, we need to heal the wounds around our inner masculine, starting with our fathers, so that we can consciously write a new script around masculinity.

Healing the Father Wound

The journey of healing the father wound is one of the most powerful journeys a woman can embark upon in her lifetime. When I say "father wound", I'm referring to a broad range of experiences from the mild wounding of a father who falls short of providing for and protecting a woman in the healthiest way, to full-blown absent or abusive fathers.

The role of the father is to provide and to protect his daughters, and to be the first male she ever loves and receives unconditional love from. The divine father archetype is also meant to provide the spiritual guidance for a woman. The father holds the masculine qualities of consciousness and acts as a sort of shining light illuminating the unconscious, as he is pure consciousness himself. He guides her when she feels lost along the path, by providing that clarity of direction and piercing penetration of a clear, neutral mind. While the mother archetype traditionally provides nurturing, nourishment, care and compassion, the father archetype supports us in developing confidence and stepping into our full strength and autonomy. If the core foundation of fatherly love and support is absent, this will very likely show up in our relationships with men later in life. A woman will begin to unconsciously project her father wound onto the men in her life. If a woman doesn't feel loved, seen, and appreciated by her father, her standards for the men in her life will be very low. She will hold the belief, "I'm unworthy of male love, so I will just settle for less than I know I truly deserve."

Think about how many women you know who grew up with fathers who were fully present, both physically and emotionally.

I can count on one hand the number of women I know who fall into this category. Many of us have fathers who provided financially, but lacked in the emotional department; or they might have been present emotionally, but failed to provide safety and basic support for the family. It's rare to find a woman who was raised by a man who was able to provide both financially and emotionally for the family and his daughters. In most cases, something was lacking. This is not to say there aren't any women who experienced healthy fathering, but it is unfortunately a lot rarer in our generation. It is my deepest desire for this to shift dramatically as more men today are doing the inner work and striving to be more conscious men and consequently, fathers.

In my case, my father provided financially but completely lacked emotional, spiritual and physical presence. Even my book doula, after reading my backstory in an earlier draft of this book, asked me, "Where was your father in all of this? You barely mention him." The truth is that I don't recall many memories of my father being in my physical presence when I was a child. My father worked in the Navy, so he would spend half the year out at sea, and the other half back with us at our family home. But when he was home, I remember that his energy was always one of anticipation for his next trip. It was like he never fully unpacked his bags when he returned, because he couldn't wait to get back out to sea. He also happened to be an alcoholic, so while he was sometimes physically present at home, he was almost always spiritually and energetically absent, as was evident in his glassy boozy-glazed eyes, sometimes as early as 10am. I remember one day he left his "coffee mug" in the kitchen and I picked it up to take it out to him on the porch. I tried to sneak in a little sip of his "coffee" only to discover that it wasn't in fact coffee—it was red wine!

There was a vicious cycle between my dad's drinking and my parents' marital problems. Things were not good between them. As young as I can remember, they would fight—and I'm not talking about a little bickering here and there, I'm talking full-blown explosions of screaming and violence, resulting in neighbors calling the police. This was a weekly occurrence. I rarely made friends with our neighbors because I felt so ashamed that the entire street could hear the whaling screams of my mother, slamming doors and often breaking objects. It wasn't long before the cops would be knocking on our door. I sensed that my Dad hated being at home, so he drowned his unprocessed trauma and emotions in alcohol, passing the time in a daze until his next departure date.

As young children, we have a natural tendency to believe that we are the cause of the events going on around us. Naturally, I internalized my Dad's unhappiness at home and made his behavior mean something about me. From his detached and resentful demeanor, I created a story of: *My father doesn't want to be around me, and I am a burden upon him.* This is a belief that ran throughout my entire adult life interacting with men, until I finally healed it. I carried this core wound of feeling that I was a burden on any man; I was too much for them. I was deeply ashamed of myself and felt that somehow I was causing pain in their lives, just like I thought I did with my father. Unsurprisingly, I spent years attracting unavailable men, narcissists who reaffirmed my core beliefs about men. It came to a pivotal moment when I knew I'd had enough of this pattern playing out. It was after my final narcissistic boyfriend pushed me to the limit, causing me to question my reality after he would gaslight me. He would make fun of me in front of his friends and then deny he ever said anything of the sorts, never apologizing, but rather twisting the situation to his favor to where I ended up apologizing for causing *him* disruption. I had had enough, so I decided to go to the root cause, to my father and get to know who my father actually is, in an attempt to heal some of these core patterns and beliefs shaping my relationship with men.

In my late-20s, I felt called to spend some time living in Perth, Australia where I was born and where my father lived at the time, to actually get to know who this man was. I realized that all I knew of him was the absent man who paid our bills and provided all the essentials we had as a family. I knew him through the lens of my mother, and her disappointments and resentments towards him. But I didn't actually know who this man was. This time of living close to him, and meeting for weekly catch-ups, was an important time of healing for me. Something I discovered then was that he never actually wanted to work in the Navy away from us, but that he felt pressured by the demands of the family to work that job in order to provide. He actually hated being away from his kids. For the first time, he shared with me so vulnerably about how he felt he had failed us as a father because he was never truly there. He was trying his best but was struggling deeply in his relationship with my mother, which made it hard for him to be present for us. All these years later, I discovered that he had never actually 'abandoned' me and my siblings, as my story of my childhood had always held. Instead, he did what he had to do to take care of us and oblige my mother, who he naturally resented as a result. This was a huge realization, as 25+ years of a false narrative crumbled before my very eyes. I didn't know whether to be happy or sad. I was happy that the belief was not actually true about my father's view of me, but also sad that I had wasted so many years believing an absolute lie and missing out on getting to know the real man who was my father. Either way, it was a key piece in healing my relationship with my father that I share to illustrate how we often hold onto these stories for far too long. I believe it's better late than never to get to the truth of the matter.

The reason I share this is because one of the most important keys to forgiving our parents—a necessary and unavoidable part of the healing path—is recognizing that the stories we formed based on our childhood perceptions of how our parents felt about us (and what we took that to mean) are often false. When we can realize this, we can finally liberate ourselves from the stories that may have imprisoned us for our entire adult life up until this point, sabotaging our relationships with men.

Connecting with the Divine Father

Rewriting our stories about our fathers and coming to a place of acceptance and forgiveness is step one of healing the father wound. The second step is about going beyond the relationship with our human biological father to access our relationship with *the* divine father, God. If we want to heal that core relationship with the masculine, I believe that we need to go straight to the source, and reestablish our connection with God/Universe/Divine, or whatever word you choose for some higher force of pure love consciousness in masculine form. The divine daughter archetype is primary; meaning that it comes before the lover and sex priestess archetypes. We need a healthy inner daughter in order to become a fully mature lover of men. If our inner daughter is wounded and crying out for our attention, she will keep unconsciously creating situations to activate this core wound of masculine abandonment until we finally address it. If we as women didn't have the experience of feeling the unconditional love, protection and safety of our fathers, it's difficult to move into the lover archetype. Instead, when we are with future male partners, we'll default back into little girl and daughter archetype, searching for a man to become the missing father we long for. My sense is that this dynamic plays a significant role in the BDSM world with the kink fetish of calling your partner "daddy" and finding arousal in being his "good obedient little girl."

This is where the Divine Father comes in. It's not your human flesh-and-blood biological dad that you need to heal the wounded daughter archetype with. It's *the* divine father—whatever expression of him resonates for you. It's about embodying the divine daughter archetype and feeling the deepest possible unconditional love and connection from source; from the father energy of life that is always guiding and protecting you. It's about knowing that you are safe, held and loved as a daughter of life itself. I believe this may have explained my fascination with God when I was as young as six years old. I wasn't feeling the fatherly energy I craved and needed from my biological human father, so I was seeking it from the big guy himself.

While I've always felt connected to a greater force beyond myself, it wasn't until an initiation in my late 20s that I fully came to embody the divine daughter archetype. A couple years after my trip to the tantric ashram, I found myself in India again, this time at a Hare Krishna ashram. This is where I experienced the divine father channeled through the form of the Krishna consciousness. The energy of Krishna is one of pure devotion. To me, it felt like the love of the father who had boundless love and joy for all his children. He was an overflow of joy and unconditional love. The level of devotion I felt to Krishna, pure *Bhakti* love flowing through me seemingly endlessly, was profound. It certainly helped that I was in the place believed to be Krishna's birthplace, the little village of Vrindavan in northern India. Every morning across the village, people would get onto their rooftops at sunrise and pray to Krishna with the deepest reverence and gratitude. The people of Vrindavan truly lived in devotion to Krishna, with temples on every street, including a 24-hour Kirtan temple where people go to chant his name, evoking his divine presence, around the clock. Everyone in Vrindavan wears traditional dress and is expected to have their prayer beads on them at all times, to be constantly chanting his name and evoking his energy of pure fatherly divine love at all times into the energetic field. I remember feeling disoriented for my first week there, because there was so much energy concentrated in my heart space, and completely out of my head space. While I don't advocate for the Kare Krishna movement, or any institutional religion for that matter, what I do support—and what I experienced there in Vrindavan—is discovering your own connection with the energy of the divine. This, I feel, is the most intimate relationship you will ever be in, and no one can tell you how this looks. Only you know. Nowadays my connection to the divine looks different from chanting Hare Krishna. It is more about running my own eros, sublimating it into the higher centers, and opening my channel to pure consciousness to flow through me. It is my primary relationship with the divine masculine and it is ever-evolving.

This experience gave me an embodied experience of the fatherly love, acceptance and protection I always longed for and knew was possible—from the true and only father archetype. It was a completion of the healing process that began with my time in Perth, reconnecting with my father and rewriting my old childhood stories about him. The impact of that was to release my expectation for every man in my life to fulfill that role, allowing me to finally operate in lover/partner energy rather than subconscious daughter/daddy energy.

In this next section, I'm going to guide you through a three-step process of beginning to heal your relationship with your father. I have used this exact process with thousands of women and, of course, for my own healing. There are three phases:

1. Becoming aware of the father wound
2. Self-validation for liberation
3. Rewriting your story about the masculine

1. *Becoming aware of the father wound*

The first step in healing anything is coming to awareness and acceptance that something is not working for you. For example, if you keep attracting unavailable men, or men that do not respect you, stop asking what is wrong with them. The empowered question is looking within yourself, without judgment, and shining a light on the parts of *you* that are running patterns that are attracting these types of men in the first place. And yes, it almost always comes back to your relationship with your father and the beliefs you formed about men from this relational dynamic. Acknowledging the pain you may have experienced as a young girl with your father opens up the gateway for transformation and healing to take place. When we become aware of the core issues and patterns, we can choose to create a new and more empowering story for ourselves moving forward.

We are going to go to the root of it all: your relationship to your father. We are starting here because to truly embody your fullness in your sexuality and feminine power, you must come to a place of wholeness within, and this always starts with your relational wounds. These relational wounds begin with our parents and it is our responsibility as adults now to heal these wounds and call back all fragmented parts of ourselves, in order to come into union with the masculine, both within and externally.

To start the process of bringing greater awareness to your father wound, reflect upon the following journal prompts:

- Overall, how happy are you with your relationship with your father?
- How was your relationship with your father growing up?

- What memories can you recall of feeling *unseen* by your father?
- What memories can you recall of feeling *seen* by your father?
- What did your father criticize about you?
- How would you have liked your father to acknowledge you?
- What did your father do that hurt you as a child?
- Was your father either physically, emotionally and/or energetically absent in your childhood? What memories arise for you about his absence?
- Do you feel that there are any unspoken agreements you made with your father?
- How do these unspoken agreements affect your relationships with men?
- What were the main traits your father possessed?
- How have these traits shown up in your male partners?
- What story have you been telling yourself about men, based on your father?

2. Self-validation for liberation

One of the main reasons we don't heal from childhood wounding and trauma is because there was minimal or no validation for our emotional state as a child. For example, maybe your father left for a work trip. In your mind, you thought he was leaving *you*, and so you began to feel sad, confused and hurt. Instead of listening and validating your emotional experience, maybe your mother just said, *Cheer up*, or *Don't be sad, just go and play with your friends*. Every time our emotions are not validated as children, it creates even more shame around the initial emotional response and pushes the emotional energy even further down in the subconscious, until we are finally able to validate our own experience fully (or to experience validation with the support of a therapist, healer or trusted friend). All we ever needed in those moments as children was to be witnessed, acknowledged and validated for our experience, not shuffled along to another state of inauthentic expression. This breeds inauthenticity and a lack of emotional intelligence in adulthood.

This is often the entire reason we hire a therapist or counselor: to literally hold space and validate our authentic emotional expression. Interestingly, this is also a divine masculine trait—the capacity to hold space and to witness without judgment. It is what we long for in our father and therefore our male partners. What we want to learn how to do is to provide validation for ourselves, embodying the father archetype of witnessing without judgment. Many of us lack this masculine quality, and when someone is upset, they try to fix them or move them along to another more joyful state of being, without allowing the person to simply have their experience. (We also do this to ourselves!) Only when we have witnessed these places within ourselves can we truly witness another in a way that is healing.

Try using these journal prompts to support your self-validation process:

- Recall the most painful experience you had with your father: one where you felt abandoned, ignored, upset, etc. Write out this experience in detail.
- Name the emotion you were experiencing at the time, or whatever is arising for you right now. Where do you feel this in your body right now?
- At the time, did you feel validated in your emotional expression?
- What would you have needed to feel validated? What would you want someone to say or do for you?

- How can you now validate what you experienced as a child? (Maybe you need to allow yourself to cry, hear some affirming words from your inner father, or offer yourself some healing touch.)
- To go deeper into this process, use some of the ***Emotional Alchemy*** tools from code 1.

3. Rewriting your story about the masculine

Now we get to the good stuff: rewriting your story about the masculine. This is where you get to step away from victim mentality and into creator mentality. What kind of reality do you want to create with men moving forward? Stepping away from the stories that have been running in the unconscious and into a more empowered place is true alchemy, where we no longer let our past define our future. It's easier said than done, I know, but like all alchemy, it is an art and requires discipline, devotion and dedication to see powerful results.

The problem with these old stories and beliefs is that they are unconscious and automatic; they come up without you even thinking about them. Reprogramming these olds beliefs is about acknowledging them, feeling them, purging them, alchemising them and then creating new stories. We want to clear out the old to make way for the new. The first step is to weed out the old beliefs around the masculine that no longer serve you.

Start by writing out all the beliefs that you are currently holding around the masculine. Some examples may be "The masculine is unreliable," "The masculine is not safe" or "The masculine does not see me." For every belief listed that evokes a strong emotion, use the emotional alchemy process to purge the emotion out of your body: identify where the emotion resides, breathe into it, and feel the emotion fully. Give it an expression—scream, yell, cry, move around, shake it out, dance, let the emotion express and purge through your cells. Go wild! Purge out all that anger, disappointment, sadness and rage.

Once you feel complete, the next step is to write out a new empowering story around the masculine. For every negative belief, directly next to it, you will write out a new, positive empowering belief. If one of your negative beliefs was "men are unreliable," the new empowering belief is "men are reliable." or "I attract reliable men." Once you've come up with all your new empowering beliefs, the next step is to record yourself speaking these beliefs into a voice memo. Listen to this before you go to bed every night for the next 21 days to anchor the new empowering beliefs into your subconscious as you sleep.

Discovering Your Inner Masculine

We've explored two kinds of relationship with the masculine: our relationship with the divine masculine/God/Source/pure consciousness, and our relationship with our biological father. Now it is time to look at our relationship with the masculine energy within. As women, our relationship with the inner masculine generally stems from our relationship with source and with our father. That's why starting with these two relationships is always the first place to begin before we can move on to healing the inner masculine.

Developing a healthy relationship with your own inner masculine then begins by establishing, *Who is this masculine archetype that I'm playing out?* Is he a lazy slob bro, an arrogant dude, a frat boy, an impotent hero, a boss, a mature man, a magician, a warrior? When I was a teenager, I used to play a game with my best friend, with no awareness that what I was doing was an actual inner masculine healing practice. It turns out that this "game" was incredibly healing, and it became the basis for my inner masculine work for women. In this game, my best friend and I would dress up as boys and act like boys, doing all sorts of crazy things as our boy alter-egos, including some things I am not proud of, like vandalizing public property and taking our parents' car for a spin around the neighborhood without licenses or even knowing how to drive a car. We would record ourselves on good old handheld cameras, playing out all these various skits and giving our inner masculine energy an expression.

We both had emotionally absent fathers, and I think what we were really doing was trying to connect to the masculine energy that was lacking at home. Like most teenage boys with absent fathers, we were rebellious and even turned to crime (although in our case it was very petty crime!). It felt like we were really expressing this energy within ourselves that wanted to be expressed and healed. It turns out, this was the therapy I needed when I revisited my inner masculine 10 years later. When I was 26, I attended a sacred sexuality retreat where one of the exercises was to dress up as our contra-sexual selves—the men dressed up as the woman living inside of them, and the women dressed up as a the man living inside of them. At the time, I hadn't consciously done work with my inner masculine for the past decade (not since my shenanigans with my best friend as a teenager), so I didn't know who my inner masculine archetype was. Through this exercise, I realized that my inner masculine was still frozen as a really immature teenage boy, like the one I used to play dress up as a teenage girl. He hadn't grown up at all. He was still a bit of a punk and rebel without a cause. In this exercise, playing him out theatrically in front of 30 strangers on the retreat, I felt a lot of shame around him. It was a little embarrassing! At this point in my life, I was an adult on a journey of becoming a conscious and empowered woman, and yet here I was finding that part of myself was still in some way a douchebag 15-year-old boy.

This was one of the most powerful practices I did to understand the masculine energy living inside of me. The second time around, I was a bit more conscious than back in my teenage days, which meant that I could actually begin to evolve this immature masculine energy inside of me. Now, I always have the women on my retreats do a similar exercise for integrating the shadow aspects of the masculine within. The biggest key to 'growing up' this inner masculine energy as a woman is not to shame him. Most of the time, the inner masculine inside a woman is actually pretty young and immature, because it is not the archetype we are living in consciously; rather, it's largely unconscious. As women, we are mostly living consciously as a female energy. One of the biggest things that helped me and also my clients to evolve their inner masculine is to bring compassion from your inner feminine for him exactly where he is at. Like any young person who is still learning and growing, they need to be embraced for exactly who and where they are in order to evolve and mature to the next stage of their development.

The place to start is by getting to know your inner masculine, which can take a little digging and self-reflection. Typically, our inner masculine holds both positive qualities that we embrace in ourselves as well as shadow qualities that we reject both in ourselves and in men in general.

Whether it's rage or inconsistency or immaturity, the qualities that you judge and reject in men are actually the keys to identifying the hidden dynamics of your own inner masculine. A powerful practice that we've done in many of my in-person Embodied Feminine Leadership Trainings is embodying the shadow aspect of your inner masculine by fully dressing up in that character and letting this energy run through your body so that it can be felt on an embodied level and then alchemized without judgment. For example, if you judge dominant men, or floaty men, or fuck boys—and you're honest enough to be able to recognize their qualities within yourself—the practice is to dress up as the masculine energy you most reject and create a short skit embodying this character. This exercise is a lot of fun and extremely healing at the same time, because the women get to feel exactly what energy they have been judging in the masculine and realize that this energy lives somewhere inside of them—they just needed an outlet of healthy expression in order to be liberated. This is Shadow Work 101: anything that we judge or shame in others is usually something we are judging or shaming within ourselves. When we can fully embody that energy instead of suppressing it down and projecting our judgment of it onto others, we shift it from the dark of the unconscious to the light of awareness, where it no longer holds power over us.

The invitation now is to allow yourself the freedom of expression to embody the qualities you've judged and rejected in men. Dress up in this character, give him a name and create a short skit. You can do this with a few friends or just do it for yourself and maybe make a short video. What you do with it is completely up to you. Journal about the experience afterwards and make note of any insights.

Bringing the Inner Masculine Into Balance

If you are holding onto a wounded relationship with the masculine, it will generally manifest in one of two possible scenarios with your own inner masculine. The first is a collapsed/absent inner masculine, and second is a hyper-masculine or dominating inner masculine energy. In the first case, a woman is lacking the masculine energy within her and looking for a man outside of her to be everything she didn't get from her father.

In the second case, she's over-developed her own masculine energy to the extent that she becomes her own man and crowds out her own inner feminine. Both are rooted in a rejection of the masculine which comes from a feeling of betrayal or abandonment from God first and foremost, and from her father secondarily. Until her relationship to the masculine is healed, she cannot enter the final stage of the mature feminine, which must be embodied in order to fully activate the Sex Priestess archetype. The priestess's power depends on a healthy relationship with both the inner and outer masculine.

The Collapsed/Absent Masculine

How does the collapsed masculine energy manifest in women? Most commonly, I see it in the archetype of the wounded maiden who demands and feels a sense of entitlement from men. A woman stuck in this archetype feels that men "owe her." She has rejected her own internal masculine and therefore struggles to hold her own, provide for herself or take care of herself, and her boundaries tend to be very weak. She throws tantrums (in her head or out loud) when she doesn't get what she wants from the men in her life.

This usually shows up in women who had abusive or controlling fathers or other significant male figures in their early life that caused them to develop a fear of masculine energy and subconsciously reject within themselves. She will likely carry anger towards the masculine and feelings of being wronged by men—hence the entitlement and conviction that men owe her something. This woman often struggles to make her own money and find direction in her life. As a result, she externalizes and projects the absent man inside of her to the outer man, looking for someone to fill this void and expecting him to take care of her, in a father-daughter or sugar daddy-baby dynamic. This is a very dysfunctional relational dynamic, as she expects and takes from him and doesn't give much in return because she is too focused on getting her own needs met. She feels he owes her for letting her down as a child.

The relationships of the wounded maiden with an absent inner masculine are dysfunctional and co-dependent, with unhealthy power dynamics at play. Her work is to develop her inner masculine so that she can fill this void of absence within herself and stop looking to fill it externally. How can she do that? The key is to go into the shadow aspects that she rejected in her father that felt "dangerous" to her—qualities of being controlling, dominant, rageful, or even abusive.

If you recognize the collapsed/absent masculine dynamic within yourself, what you need to work on is embracing those "dangerous" qualities that could very well be living inside of you, adopted from your father, but manifesting in some distorted version that you might not recognize. You might be completely dissociated from these qualities from suppressing and rejecting them. But for the most part, when we deny any parts of ourselves, they almost always come out sideways. You may be rejecting this dominating aspect that lives inside of you for fear of being like your father, but it could actually be coming out as manipulative energy instead. Or your rejection of your father's rage might come out as passive aggression. The key is to recognize the root quality and alchemize it into its highest expression. For example, there is nothing wrong with dominance. A shadow or distorted relationship to dominance might come out in wanting to be dominated or being submissive. But when alchemized into its highest expression, healthy dominance is more like authority—the quality of a great leader and leadership in general. You could use this quality to dominate your own fear and self-doubt, for instance, or to command an audience's attention when you're speaking to a group. Likewise, if you've been suppressing your rage, you've probably also been suppressing your will and creative power. Rage can be alchemized into passion, drive and will power. Control, likewise, can be alchemized into discipline and focus. All powerful aspects of the masculine expression live inside of us, and they can be unlocked in ways that support our feminine being and our work in the world.

Self-inquiry

1. Write out all the qualities in your father that you felt were unattractive or undesirable. Then, next to each of these qualities, write out the alchemized highest expression of that quality.
2. Next, get honest about how these qualities play out for you and how you can embody the highest expression of the qualities more in your life. For example, where can you be more disciplined, passionate or assertive in your life?

The Hyper-Masculine

The other expression of the imbalanced inner masculine is the hyper-masculine overcompensating energy within a woman. In this case, instead of rejecting the masculine qualities within herself, she *overdevelops* them. This manifests as the classic career woman, "boss babe" archetype; the woman who essentially becomes her own man. She provides for herself and protects herself to the point that she doesn't really know what role a man would play in her life anymore because her inner masculine is running the show and doing a pretty good job. This energy manifests as hyper-driven, goal-oriented, assertive/aggressive and ruthless in business. This woman has her masculine side very highly developed, but generally it is at the expense of her inner feminine. What is going on internally, is her inner masculine is taking the forefront of her consciousness and overshadowing her feminine qualities. She may have adopted this masculine archetype due to conditioning in her childhood that led her to believe that feminine qualities are weaker, and inferior to her masculine qualities. As a result, her femininity becomes suppressed and stifled because so much of her energy, attention and identity goes into her masculine side, which she relies on to get shit done, make money, provide for herself and protect herself. Deep down, this woman typically longs to relinquish control and surrender to a man, but all the armor she has built up around her heart and the fortress of the empire she's built isn't allowing for men to come anywhere near her. Because her father was absent or she felt betrayed by him as a little girl, she may now find it very difficult to let down the guard of her own inner masculine protector and let any man close to her. She will often perpetuate the belief of "men will disappoint you" by attracting unavailable men and narcissists to reaffirm her inner conviction that she cannot trust men.

The hyper-masculine can also develop in situations where the woman's mother never felt the support—emotionally, energetically and even physically—from the father of her children. What happens is that the mother projects this husband she longs for from the father of her children onto the children themselves. Typically it gets projected onto the eldest, and especially the eldest son. This child innately feels a deep need to protect the mother and provide, emotionally and sometimes even financially when they are old enough. In psychological terms, this is called the "impotent hero"—the shadow aspect of the warrior archetype in which the child is forever attempting to save their mother, and then transfers this need to save onto every partner thereafter. While it happens a lot with boys, it is also common with firstborn women—including me. After countless conversations with high-achieving female clients, I have drawn parallels that many of these women also grew up with single mothers or a mother who never felt that she got what she longed for from the father of her children. What this pattern has shown me is that so much of the drive to achieve as hyper-masculine women is actually stemming from this impotent hero archetype. We're trying to win our mother's love through achievements, money and status, and yet never feeling like we're good enough or we've done enough.

The key here is allowing the impotent hero, trying to save everyone else, to die, and becoming your own hero. Let go of the need for approval from your mother and others, and start self-validating and living from a deeper place of inner authority. There also has to be a disconnect of the energetic umbilical cord between you and your mother, which will help you release any guilt and psychological responsibility that you may be unconsciously carrying that is not yours to carry. This process also involves connecting to your own womb as a woman (tapping into and embodying the mother-creator archetype within you) and plugging into the divine mother who is the womb of life and the body of the earth. This is another benefit of the work we did in Code 1 to awaken the womb. The inner masculine and feminine are deeply connected and interdependent, so working on one also supports the other, as we'll learn more in Code 3. When a woman becomes fully embodied in her feminine power, she begins to evolve her inner masculine energy from the impotent hero that never feels good enough to the hero of her own life and thus more mature masculine energy.

To be clear, there is nothing wrong with being a boss and career woman with strong masculine qualities. But what you want to consider is whether you are denying your feminine desire for love, connection and intimacy as a result of being overly focused on your masculine energy as a way to protect yourself from getting hurt by men. Women who have over-developed masculine energy often actually have unhealthy masculine energy.

It's not so different from a man who is solely focused on his business and has no time for a relationship or love—he values his personal mission, money and success over relationships and feels that a woman will distract him from his single-pointed focus on his career goals. This is often what is unconsciously playing out in a woman who feels that relationships are a distraction from her career. Deep down in the core of her feminine essence, she longs for partnership. When we embody more of the healthy masculine, we realize that intimacy, partnership and relationships can actually *enhance* our work and support our career goals. For many women, it's not about killing her inner man who has gotten her to this point of success in her life, it's actually about growing him up into more healthy masculine energy, which includes coming into harmony with the inner feminine, who deeply values slowing down, intimacy, *being* over doing, relationships and love. I actually tell my clients who fall into this category that it's a good thing they have strong masculine energy already there, because this actually creates more of a foundation for them to drop into their healthy feminine expression, because masculine energy is what holds the feminine. For these women, it is about developing healthier masculine energy and allowing the feminine expression and her desires to be seen and heard.

Self-inquiry Practice

1. Write a list of all the most admirable masculine qualities you embody (for example, provider energy, focused, disciplined, strong, etc.)
2. From this list, expand on each quality by honestly listing all the different ways it could potentially be

expressed (for example, too focused on work, no down time, set in your ways not flexible at all to change, controlling and unable to trust anyone). Then circle which ones you feel could be unhealthy expressions of your masculine energy.
3. Next to this list, write out how you can start to mature and bring balance to those aspects of yourself that may be rooted in an unhealthy masculine expression.

Healthy Masculine, Empowered Feminine

Once you've accepted your inner masculine as it is, then you can begin to look at the mature masculine qualities qualities you aspire to embody, including: direction, drive, purpose, discipline, presence, focus, integrity, determination, authority and leadership. Start to look at HOW you can embody those qualities. For example, if presence is something you lack, maybe you need to start a mindfulness practice or go sit a 10-day silent meditation retreat. If discipline is something you lack, maybe you can hire a coach and be held accountable in working towards a specific goal with sustained, committed daily action.

Another important factor in my own inner masculine evolution has been finding male mentors who embody the healthy masculine energy I most desire to embody. Of course, this healing and evolution can also occur with the man you choose as your beloved. Hiring a male coach or seeking out male friends to be surrounded by high-caliber mature male energy is incredibly healing for women who are desiring to embody their healthy inner masculine and cultivate better relationships with men.

When a woman has healed her inner masculine, she can hold and provide for herself, but at the same time, she allows herself to be held by worthy, mature men and also by the divine masculine

(God). The natural template for a woman, a womb-bearing human, is to surrender completely to the masculine, to be led by his pure aligned consciousness. This applies to both her own inner masculine and also to the external masculine. A woman who has developed her own inner masculine will always desire an external masculine who is much more evolved and more masculine than her own inner masculine. This is the only way she will be able to surrender and relinquish control. Surrendering to the masculine doesn't mean that we just immediately surrender to any man who comes along—no. This is not what I mean when I speak about surrendering to the masculine. Your mature woman, as feminine as she is, also holds strong discernment and access to the wise woman archetype, who knows if this man is someone to invest in getting to know and potentially eventually surrendering to.

Mature masculine energy does not need to coerce, force or dominate a woman into surrender. There is so much confusion around this in the spiritual community. When a man feels threatened by the feminine, he feels the need to "dominate" her. For both genders, this is a psychological trait called an inferiority complex: one feels powerless and so seeks to gain power over others. What we see in our society has been thousands of years of this dynamic playing out between men and women. Dominate the feminine, because we fear the feminine. So much of this is also playing out in the spiritual/polarity/tantra teachings, which I feel is yet another form of patriarchy cloaked as "relational teachings." Usually it takes the form of male teachers teaching women how to be more feminine by 'submitting' to a man in the name of 'devotion'. Don't get me wrong, I am all about devotion, but being a good little girl is not what being a mature woman or devotion feels like. Instead, this is the little girl with unresolved father wounds, appeasing her father to gain his love and approval, who never received the guidance and support she longed for from her father.

When I feel into the mature masculine-feminine dynamic, a mature woman does not 'submit' to a mature man; rather, she consciously surrenders. These two energies are sovereign and because the mature man is secure in himself and there is no need to dominate the mature woman. She simply trusts and can effortlessly surrender to his lead, because he is holding utmost presence, integrity, power and awareness. I recently had an experience with a much older man that deepened me into what true, healthy masculine-feminine felt like in a relationship. Not once did I hear the words dom/sub. Because he was so secure in himself and his masculinity, I naturally surrendered and trusted him. However, I still felt incredibly empowered in my voice, seen and heard in my own leadership and feminine power. I was never once made to feel like a little girl to his dominance, in order to make him feel a sense of power through gaining power over me. When you feel the thrust into your mature woman, from a mature man, you will know. It's a very clear, strong inner knowing. It takes having that discernment of your feminine oracle to decide if he is worthy of your surrender. Your inner masculine will feel safe to step to the side to give the external masculine a chance of entering your heart and space. Your inner masculine sets the boundaries and your inner feminine sets the pace through leading the direction with her desires. For example, you will express a desire to connect more intimately with this man, if you so authentically feel this and feel into what feels good for you at this point in the dynamic. You may just feel good with kissing and cuddling, and your inner masculine sets the boundaries and sticks to them in integrity. Each desire is expressed authentically from your feminine, and then you can see if this man can actually meet you there or not. If he cannot respect your boundaries or the pace that feels authentic to you as the feminine initiator, you let him go.

Healing our inner masculine as a female-bodied being is one of the core aspects of tantra. Once we feel we have made peace with our biological father, *the* divine father God, and consequently our inner masculine, is when we find ourselves on the path of true union. First inner union must take place in order for outer union to truly manifest. This is what we will explore in the next code, *Inner Union*.

CODE 3:
INNER UNION

Not only within men and women but all of life exists in polarities of masculine and feminine. These polarities can exist in a state of tension and conflict with one another, or in a state of balance, harmony and ultimately, union. Tantra is the path of merging opposites into a greater union, bringing healing, awakening and higher consciousness in the process. This happens on an energetic and bodily level within ourselves as well as on the level of the soul and psyche. Before we unite with another, we must find true union within ourselves.

This next code is all about creating harmony within yourself through inner union of the masculine and feminine. We are always seeking a state of equilibrium internally and also in our outer world, for this is when we feel most at ease. The most common place we seek union is in partnerships, through merging male and female polarities with another. Yet the true union comes when we have found this merging of masculine and feminine polarities within ourselves. The Greeks called this *hieros gamos*, the "sacred marriage" between a god and goddess. This union of opposites is also the highest stage of the alchemical process and the ultimate goal of alchemy. Psychoanalyst Carl Jung described the soul's journey of individuation as a process of evolving towards an inner marriage of the mature masculine and the mature feminine. Of course, true union with another human being can only take place when we have married these opposing forces within.

Jung speaks extensively about the terms "anima" and "animus" as part of his theory of the collective unconscious—the universe principles and archetypes of the human psyche. He described the animus as the unconscious masculine side of a woman, and the anima as the unconscious feminine side of a man. Whatever lies in the unconscious holds power over you. To become whole and fully integrated as women, we must come into union with the masculine side (animus) and for men, it's about doing the same with their feminine side (anima).

In my days studying tantric philosophy at the Ashram in India, I learned that Carl Jung was actually very well studied in the tantric philosophies of Shiva/Shakti and he brought tantric teachings through a psychological lens to the masses. I believe the Anima/Animus work was definitely one of these teachings. Tantra is about balancing these polarities within us, and in doing so, coming into union externally in our relationships. Let's take a closer look at the tantric philosophy of masculine-feminine polarity and sacred union.

Tantric energetics and union

To get started, we'll look at a tantric perspective on the inner union and how this operates on an energetic level. This will give you a broader sense of what inner union really means before we bring it down into the earthly, personal and relational dimension.

Sacred union is the fundamental essence of tantra and yoga. The greater aim of tantric and yogic practices is to bring ourselves into union. This is what all the yoga postures are about, bringing the energy channels into perfect harmony so that our life force can flow freely. Certain breathing practices, like nadi shodhana, are specifically designed to bring the left and right hemisphere of the brain into perfect balance and harmony. Beyond male and female and what makes a man a man, and a woman a woman, what tantra and yoga are designed to do is to bring these universal principles of sun and moon, yin and yang, shakti and shiva, masculine and feminine into harmony within us. How this manifests internally is through the two main energetic channels, or *nadis*, that run up and down the spine. In the energy body, there are 72,000 energy channels or *nadis*. The 72,000 nadis all spring from three basic nadis – the left, the right and the central channel – the Ida, Pingala, and Sushumna. Nadis are pathways or channels of *prana*, life force energy, in the system. If you cut the body and take a look inside, you will not see the 72,000 nadis as they don't have a physical manifestation but rather are invisible energy channels. However, they can be linked to the anatomy of the nervous system. But as you become more aware, you will notice that energy is not moving at random; it's moving along established pathways. There are 72,000 different ways in which the energy or *prana* moves.

All yoga and tantra practices are about balancing these energy channels or *nadis* so that our life force can flow in perfect harmony. The central channel, or sushumna, which runs directly through the center of the spine, is where our kundalini or *shakti* energy runs up and down. When in perfect harmony, this energy is free-flowing, and we naturally unlock our fullest human and spiritual potential.

If you know anything about the anatomy of the spine, you're aware that there are two holes on either side of the spine which are like conduit pipes for all the nerves to pass. This is the Ida and the Pingala, the left and the right channels. The Ida is said to be the feminine or lunar channel, and the pingala is the masculine or solar channel. The Ida and Pingala represent the basic duality of all of existence. It is this duality which is traditionally personified as Shiva and Shakti, or masculine and feminine, or you might think of it as the logical and the intuitive aspects of yourself. It is out of this duality that life is created. Without these two dualities, life wouldn't exist as it does right now.

In the beginning, before we incarnate to this physical dimension, we are pure source consciousness, formless, timeless, and spaceless. Everything is primordial; there is no duality. But once creation happens and we incarnate into this physical dimension, there is duality. Conception happens when a sperm (masculine) unites with an egg (feminine) for the beginnings of a new life to form. So in order to come into perfect union, with this essential life force flowing up the central channel, we want to bring these two channels into harmony. I believe that this connects us back to source primordial energy. When we feel this energy running up our spine on the vertical plane, back to unity consciousness, beyond duality, we remember where we came from and who we truly are. This is yoga. This is tantra.

What most of us are experiencing, unfortunately, is not this state of union and harmony. More often, what we experience is the essential life force energy running predominantly up either one side or the other. This is where major imbalances occur within our energetic being. Too much energy flowing up the solar pingala channel creates too much fire within us, like the sun. An example of this is the experience of literal burnout from overdoing, over-achieving, and pushing yourself too far beyond your capacity, which is unfortunately extremely common. This energy is like a wildfire that can be very destructive in one's life. Fire is essential for our energy and vitality, but in excess, we run ourselves into the ground.

Too much energy flowing up the lunar ida channel creates too much water within us, like the moon. Having too much water in one's energetic makeup can lead you to be overly emotional to the point of feeling like you are drowning your emotions and have no control over them. You may also experience feeling too flowy like water, lacking any clear direction. Water is a force that, when in balance, moves energy and allows us to have a healthy flow of emotions. But like all elements, when in excess, it becomes destructive, causing emotional overwhelm and aimlessness.

When kundalini flows up one of these channels too quickly, there is a potential for us to experience extreme imbalances in our psyche. I believe this is what happened to me as a 14-year-old. Much of what we see as mental illnesses like bipolar, schizophrenia and even depression, I truly believe is simply an imbalance of this essential life force moving through a blocked channel and not able to flow freely through the central channel. Because when the kundalini blasts up one channel only and reaches all the way to the crown, it will spin very fast in the third eye. Too much energy circulating in the third eye in an imbalanced way can create all sorts of mental and psychological imbalances, including delusions, false perceptions and paranoia. For our own safety and stability, we really want to ensure that the two opposing energetic channels within us are in harmony before attempting to awaken our kundalini. This is what all yoga asanas and pranayama are designed for. It's about balancing out the 72,000 energy channels or nadis in the body, so the kundalini can awaken slowly and gracefully up the central channel and not in a rush or in a scattered and off-kilter manner. This is why tantra and yoga was such a saving grace for me. When I understood these energetic dynamics, I finally had an explanation and context for what happened to me at 14. This is why I'm so passionate about these practices as foundations for us as humans awakening our fullest potential—for real, in these sensitive physical vessels, not by trying to blast ourselves into higher consciousness in a way that is not healthy or balanced.

Meeting in the Heart Space

These energy channels flowing through our being come together to form seven main energy centers, which we know as *chakras*. There's a good chance you're already very familiar with the chakras, but to give a short summary: Each of the seven chakras governs certain organs and psychological functions around it. We have the first root chakra located at the base of the spine, which is linked to our survival, sense of safety and connection to tribe. It governs our elimination organs and what blocks this chakra is fear. Then we have the second chakra, the sacral, located just below the naval which is linked to our sexuality, creativity and expression. It governs the reproductive organs. What blocks this chakra is shame, guilt and unworthiness. Then we have the third, solar plexus chakra, located just above the naval, which is linked to our sense of power, will power and authority. It governs the digestive organs and stomach; what blocks this chakra is anger and powerlessness. Then we have the fourth, the heart chakra, located at the heart, governing the heart organ and lungs, and thus our sense of compassion, unconditional love and joy. What blocks it is grief and sadness. Next we have the fifth, the throat chakra, located at the physical throat, governing the thyroid function and our ability to speak our truth, self-confidence and expression. It becomes blocked by depression, anxiety and low self-esteem. Next we have the sixth, the third eye chakra, located in between the eyebrows, governing clarity, intuition, imagination, universal connection, spiritual perception, concentration. What blocks it is ignorance, pessimism, lack of purpose, uncertainty and confusion. The final, seventh chakra is the crown chakra and this energy center controls your connection to spirit, as well as your sense of universal consciousness, wisdom, unity, and self-knowledge. What blocks it is shallow relationships, fear of change, repressed emotions and inflated ego.

In this energetic system, you can see we have seven chakras in total—three upper and three lower, with the center point being the heart chakra. The lower three chakras, the root, sacral and solar plexus, are representative of the feminine or manifest/material dimension, represented by a downward triangle. And the upper three chakras, the throat, third eye and crown, are representative of the masculine or pure consciousness dimension, represented by an upward triangle. In the center is the heart space, the melting pot of all duality, where the lower earthly feminine primal aspects of our being merge with the upper masculine divine aspects. This is where logos and eros meet, where feminine and masculine meet, where all polarities and dualities unite, is in the heart space. This is why opposites attract, why God created us as two opposites of the spectrum, and why love is the most powerful force that calls us back into true unity consciousness.

When we experience the free flow of energy up the central channel sushumna, it eventually dwells and makes its way into the heart space; into unity. This is often experienced as a feeling of inner peace, which comes from feeling very balanced in one's opposing energies. When the two opposing forces meet at the heart space, we experience an overflow of positive energy and a deep desire to love, to be of service, and to give our gifts to the world. This, I believe, is the ultimate goal of tantra and yoga. This is where we long to live from, in union with the different parts of ourselves, with other people, and with all of life. This is what it's all about. We want to experience ourselves as one with all duality, and yet return back to the state of pure unity consciousness as we live from our heart consciousness. This is why we are attracted to the opposite sex, the gender polarity to balance ourselves out, to meet in the heart space. How can we celebrate the differences on the human personality and energetic level between man and woman, and not try to change one another, but instead let natural law support us to meet in the heart space, in love?

The Lower Triangle: Embracing the Feminine Polarity by Returning to Embodiment

The unfortunate result of thousands of years of patriarchal religions and spiritual traditions is a complete disconnect from the feminine polarity—a suppression of the feminine, a denial of the material and physical dimension of life (mother/matter), shaming the body, shaming sex, shaming menstrual blood. This is in fact a denial of all aspects of the first three chakras, the feminine dimension. Any religion or philosophy that denies one half of the equation of life is not operating from unity consciousness and love, it is operating from separation and fear. Some religions make their followers wear a certain dress code that covers the legs completely, and wraps a sash around the waist just where the solar plexus starts, as a symbol of denying and hiding the primal and feminine aspect of our nature. The body, the feminine, is seen as impure and something to be ashamed of, and is believed to be completely disconnected from our divinity. This goes completely against what I know to be true, which is that we came here as pure consciousness to be fully embodied in this human experience, to express pure consciousness through this physical fleshy vessel that we call the body. This, I believe, is the gateway to liberation.

In my experience, and from a tantric perspective, liberation happens through the body. The body is the home of your soul. The most enlightening thing you can do is not to escape this flesh and bones, but rather inhabit it fully. Most institutional religions, and many spiritual practices, are about escaping the body. To truly liberate—meaning, to truly burn away one's karma and thus actually be able to ascend to higher states of consciousness—there has to be a descent into the body. After I left my body for those three days, I knew the danger of hanging out in the upper realms without a solid root and two feet on the earth plane. I know not to romanticize the pursuit of higher consciousness at the expense of being embodied and empowered on a material level. This has completely shaped my spiritual path the past 20 years of my life that I have devoted to teaching and practicing embodiment. We must feel what needs to be felt on an embodied level, because the karmas (the habitual reactions, patterns and false beliefs due to past conditioning that long to be liberated) live in the cells of your body, not in your mind. They live in your organs, your body tissue, your blood and your bones.

No one is coming to save you but yourself. If you aren't inhabiting your body, if you're floating around in your head and in the astral realms, dissociating to avoid the pain and reality of this human experience, it can really cause problems in your life. This is like leaving all the doors open to your home—anything and anyone can enter your body and your energy field. You become susceptible to all sorts of f*ckery, will struggle to have any backbone and will fall for anything. Embodiment is essential. Looking after the body is essential. Feeling is essential. This is the feminine dimension, the lower triangle, the first three chakras. To liberate ourselves, we must inhabit the body and feel what is there. The deeper we can feel the quicker it can alchemise and dissolve—more energy, wisdom, truth, light and consciousness can flood through. From there we come into harmony with our higher consciousness, the masculine principles, and merge within; in the heart space.

This might all seem very basic, especially if you have been doing inner work and on a spiritual path. But no matter how experienced you are or how much you've healed yourself, this is the ground-level foundation of awakening, feminine empowerment and embodying the sex priestess archetype that you will need to come back to again and again. If you have resistance to this or feel that you don't need to pay attention to this information because you've already mastered it, I encourage you to take another look and see where you could work on stepping into an even deeper embodiment of your lower chakras. This is a lifelong process of feminine mastery.

The Masculine Upper Triangle: From Formlessness to Form

On the other end of the spectrum is the masculine upper triangle, which resembles the upward path of ascension. This encompasses the upper three chakras above the heart: the throat, the third eye and the crown. The upward triangle is the representation of the masculine polarity, because it is one of ascending through increasing access to higher states of consciousness and awareness. When these chakras are well-developed, we cultivate the ability to see beyond duality, and even access information from other dimensions. The danger with most spiritual teachings is that they are solely focused on this path, completely disregarding the lower triangle. There is a saying, "The higher the branches, the deeper the roots." This means that the higher you ascend, the deeper you must be embodied. What is often missing is the precursor of descending first. We must anchor our roots through healing our lower three chakras and feeling safe in the body if we are to truly ascend into the higher states of consciousness, safely. This is where we get to access higher states and information beyond time and space—and then have the ability to ground that information into this reality. (And if you can't ground the information that you're receiving, then what is the point, really?) When you look at a woman who births a child, this is the ultimate embodiment of grounding higher consciousness. She receives a speck of stardust from pure Source itself and houses that child in her body, then births that child into this dimension through her yoni portal. The same can be applied to conceiving information or creative ideas. We must be the bridges as we hold this physical vessel, being firmly rooted in the body, with deep roots that allow us to fly high and then retrieve information from these other planes to anchor them in this reality, whether that is a child, an idea, a creation of any sorts. This is what our bodies are for—to be transmitters of the divine energies. We are powerful vessels of creation.

Your Biology Doesn't Lie

Now that we've explored the macro picture of your inner masculine and feminine, and how this polarity functions on a physical and energetic level, it's time to start letting this knowledge trickle down into the earth dimension, and specifically, our relationships. As you now know, we all have inner masculine and feminine energies, the ida and pingala, sun and moon, water and fire channels that run through us, that we can bring into balance, harmony and ultimately perfect unity and non-duality. However, let us remember God's perfect creation of us as man and woman. Biology still exists. You may think well if we are meant to come into perfect inner union, why would God create man and woman? But this is exactly the point: we were created in duality. This teaches us that every aspect of life is created from a balanced interaction of opposite and competing forces. Yet these forces are not just opposites; they are complementary. They do not cancel out each other. Instead, they balance each other like the dual wings of a bird.

When we look at male-bodied beings and female-bodied beings, there are some biological differences that make us opposite and complementary. Look at our genitals: a man's genitals are outward, representing the outward solar energy of penetration, while a woman's genitals are tucked inside, representing the inward lunar receptive energy. Both fit one another like a hand in a glove. They are complementary. When it comes to our hormones, male hormones are more flat, even and predictable every month, staying relatively stable like the predictable solar energy of the sun. A woman's hormones, on the other hand, are cyclical; they fluctuate by starting at a low point during menstruation, peaking during ovulation, and then taping off again in a full four-phase cycle, perfectly in sync with the four cycles of the moon (new, waxing, full and waning) and the lunar energy.

Our biology does not lie. God created us as perfect complements to one another. Therefore, we in fact need one another to balance one another out on a physical level, man and woman. This is natural law and what we were designed to come here to experience in God's perfection. Yes, a woman is more feminine in her essence and biology, and yet she still has that aspect of herself that is connected to her yang, her masculine solar energy. And man is more masculine in his essence and biology, and yet he still has that aspect of him connected to his yin, his feminine lunar energy. The goal is to find harmony within so that we can come to a place of complementing one another rather than *depending* upon one another.

The same energetics and polarity balancing applies in non-hetero relationships, whereby one partner will hold the masculine pole and the other holds the feminine pole. Yes, biology shows the same genitalia, but on an energetic level in every healthy relationship with sexual attraction, one partner will always be holding opposite ends of the spectrum of masculine and feminine. I can attest to this as I dated a woman for six months in my mid-20s and she held a very masculine energetic template—in fact, more masculine than many men I knew at the time. Through that experience, I really saw that these principles can be applied in both hetero and non-hetero relationships.

TANTRA: Balancing the Polarities Within

I see all around me that we are entering a new paradigm of relationships based upon principles of co-creation, and interdependence over codependency. When a woman enters a relationship with zero connection to her inner masculine, she will naturally project that masculine essence out upon the man and depend upon him in all the ways masculine energy manifests. That might mean that it's very difficult for her to look after herself when she's single, make her own money or have any direction in life because she solely relies upon men to meet these needs. This is what a relationship based upon codependency looks like: she depends upon him to fulfill a role that is naturally available to her as a grown woman, and thus disempowers herself. The same goes for men. If they have no connection to the feminine side of themselves they will forever project that upon every woman that enters their life, and when they are single, they cannot nurture themselves or offer themselves emotional support, and they lack erotic energy and creativity that the feminine brings into existence through her nature.

This old-paradigm dynamic of relating has evolved though as women are developing more of their healthy inner masculine energy and more men are cultivating their healthy inner feminine energy. The key is evolving these two energies within ourselves to a mature and healthy expression in order to bring them into union with one another. When this happens, two whole and complete beings get into a relationship, and they can help each other to grow and evolve from a place of wholeness rather than trying to fill something that is lacking in the other. Of course, a woman will still hold predominantly feminine qualities, and a man will have predominantly masculine qualities, but because they have access to that other side of themselves, they are coming into union as two balanced beings. Just like the yin-yang symbol, the white side has a dot of black, the black side has a dot of white. This is a reflection of the balance of energies inside of us. Then the two sides merge to create a perfect harmonic circle, two wholesome balanced beings create a third entity, the relationship circle.

When we meet with another whole person with our own inner polarities balanced, a third energy is formed between the two individuals—I like to call this the tantric energy, or force of co-creation. These two beings come together to serve a higher force, which is the relationship container itself. The divine purpose of the relationship is beyond the two personal egos. Two beings can merge into a third entity, a third force that is here to create something new with the powerful force of shiva and shakti in harmony. The couple is here to create a family, a child, a business, a community, a way of life. The purpose also extends to at its deepest core supporting each other's soul path and highest unfolding and liberation. Whatever it is, it is something beyond the personal "me." Rather, it is about serving the "we"—the relationship entity itself. This, I believe, is the true purpose of the sacred union relationship. In order to come to this highest vision, we must come into inner union within our own individual selves first.

The Journey of Inner Union

This journey of coming into inner union can be a lifelong journey of mastery, and one that I can say I am still a student of. But in my own process, I've learned a lot along the way. I have gone from feeling completely disconnected from my inner masculine, casting him very deep into the shadows, to then becoming hyper-masculine, to now resting somewhere much more balanced in between.

When we're working with any kind of polarity, we usually have to swing from one end of the spectrum to the other in order to balance ourselves out. If you never expressed boundaries in your life, then once you finally discover your boundaries, you might go to the other extreme of becoming the boundary Queen and quite rigid and closed-off from others. This may seem like a mistake, but it's actually essential in order to find the balance, and natural law dictates that we always balance out. The nature of all polarity is that it balances out in the middle eventually after swinging from one side to the other, like the movement of a pendulum. If the pendulum is very far to one side, you can guarantee it is going to swing to the other extreme as it seeks equilibrium.

In the last code, we explored the process of establishing a relationship with your inner masculine. This code is now about bringing them into harmony by creating a healthy inner dialogue. How does your inner feminine view your inner masculine? How does your inner masculine view your inner feminine? It is so important that these two come into healthy dialogue in order to create a healthy inner union. As with any relationship, good communication is key.

Imagine a relationship between a man and a woman projected outwards from inside of you, with the male aspect of you and the female aspect of you sitting face to face. What sort of relationship are they in? Is it a dysfunctional relationship, or is it a healthy relationship? Are both expressing their needs and desires? Are they being fulfilled? Or is only one party getting their needs met, and the other is left feeling neglected and resentful?

For many years, my inner masculine was at the beck and call of my inner feminine. They were in a very disharmonious relationship. At first my inner masculine was collapsed and I was just being led by my immature feminine impulse energy of floating around without any direction at all. Then once my inner masculine started to evolve and find purpose and have a sense of direction, he was being ordered around by my inner feminine and she was demanding more, more, more from him. All of my inner feminine needs were being met, but when it came to my inner masculine side, I felt he was really emasculated and playing the "good guy" trying to please my inner feminine. He had no say in what he wanted.

Nadine Lee

When I got clear on what my inner masculine desired, things like sexual exploration, travel and play were high on the list. Yet my inner feminines desires always overrode his desires, so he was working to provide the luxuries for her, but had to just settle for giving up his desire to travel and explore the world. This conflict was playing out unconsciously for many years. It's only in the past few years that I started to create an inner dialogue between the two aspects of myself, and therefore started to bring them into harmony and fulfill both of their needs.

Here's a real example: I was once invited to a play party where people were guided through intimacy and connection exercises, and invited to explore with each other. People are welcome to have sex openly if they wanted to. My inner masculine side was like, "Yes, this will be so fun to play and explore." That part of me desired freedom and spontaneous play and connection. But the feminine side of me longed for sacred union with one beloved, and requires a lot of safety in order to open up sexually, or to any level of intimacy. I felt conflicted within myself, literally as if I were being pulled in opposite directions. Without the conscious awareness of my inner dialogue, I would have let my feminine desire—which was a hard no to this party—override my masculine desire, but in this situation I allowed the two sides of me to come into a conversation and find a middle path. My feminine side needed safety, so what she needed was to call up the organizers and ask them a few questions to rest her worries at ease. Once she felt that, and had the option to express her boundaries in a healthy way, the masculine side felt free to go to the party with her, aware of her boundaries. And it turns out, nothing crazy happened. I ended up just having beautiful conversations with many different beautiful men at the party. Both sides of me felt completely satisfied—my feminine need for safety and my masculine need for freedom and exploration.

Astrological Archetypes: Working with Venus & Mars

One of the most profound tools I have used to explore and understand these two opposing forces within me on a more personality/character dimension, has been astrological archetypes—specifically, understanding where Mars and Venus are placed in your birth chart. Now I want to put a forewarning here that your inner masculine and feminine are not limited to just these archetypes, but they're a good starting point to building this inner dialogue between these two aspects of self to bring them into unity and consciousness.

In my own chart, I have Mars in Leo, ruled by the Sun, which makes so much sense when I realized that the masculine side of me felt like a Leo type of man: loud and proud, penetrative and poised. He is a provider, King energy, sometimes competitive, needs to be the best and loves being center of attention—all very Leo-type traits. My Venus is placed in Cancer, which is ruled by the moon. They are polar opposites. This made so much sense as the feminine side of me craves security, a sense of home and nurturing, and family. She is strongly driven by security and safety. My inner dialogue began by acknowledging these two strong opposing energetic forces, and making sure that my Venus (feminine) feels safe, so my Mars (masculine) can be free to roam. When I realized this, everything made sense, including the types of men I would attract when my own inner masculine was emasculated (namely, men who were also emasculated and not in their power). But once my inner union started to form, and my inner masculine was in harmony with my inner feminine, I began attracting the type of men I desired: men in their power. Often we attract men who reflect the sign of our Mars in order to learn how to embody that masculine energy and integrate it within ourselves. This also taught me why I was attracted to so many Leo men in my younger years—they were teaching me how to embody my masculine power.

Identifying your Inner Masculine & Feminine

As you've been reading this chapter, I hope you've been reflecting on the dynamics of your own inner polarities and starting to find some clarity. Now it's time to begin creating this dialogue within yourself. The first step is to identify where your Venus and Mars are placed in your own astrological chart. You can do this on any astrology website, like Cafe Astrology, that offers a free natal chart reading (you can find a link listed in the appendix at the end of the book).

- Once you've identified where your Mars and Venus are placed, feel into the archetypes of each sign and reflect on who is this inner man within you and who is this inner woman within you.
- What are the characteristics of each? If you need some inspiration, do some reading and research on the qualities of each sign, including some famous men or women born under that sign.
- In your journal, draw two columns. The left side is your inner feminine (Venus) and the right side is your inner masculine (Mars). On the left, list all the qualities of this Venus woman. Then on the right, list all the qualities of this Mars man. They may overlap quite a bit with the characteristics that you wrote above, but make sure to keep it focused on you rather than the broader astrological traits.
- Next, answer in your journal: What does the inner masculine (Mars) side of you desire the most? Does he feel supported in his desires?

- Then answer in your journal: what does the inner feminine (Venus) side of you desire the most? Does she feel supported in her desires?

Creating the Dialogue

The next step of coming into union is bringing these two opposing forces within you into harmony by creating a conscious dialogue between them. This is where you get to see what sort of relationship these two forces are in. Are they in harmony or disharmony? Is one side of you getting its needs met while the other is neglected? Is one side dominating or suppressing the other? When you bring awareness to these dynamics, you will be surprised how this shifts your entire life into more harmony, from how you operate day-to-day to how you show up in your relationships and business. The exercise below will help you create the dialogue between your inner feminine and masculine to come into inner union.

Take out your journal and answer the following questions:

- What is my inner masculine side desiring to experience today?
- What is my inner feminine side desiring to experience today?
- What does my inner masculine side need from my feminine in order to fulfill this desire?
- What does my inner feminine side need from my masculine in order to fulfill this desire?
- Then you are going to write a free-flowing conversational dialogue between the two, starting with feminine: let her write whatever wants to come through. Then respond from your masculine, let him write whatever wants to come through. Then keep going back and forth as

a dialogue conversation written down on paper until you come to a loving compromise in the middle and harmony within both sides expressing their needs, and feeling satisfied in getting them met, while honoring the other side.

Inner Marriage Ritual

You know that you are truly ready for marriage when you have married yourself; essentially, you have come to complete inner union of your masculine and feminine polarities. When both of these sides feel they are being nourished by the other, versus at war with one another is when we feel a sense of wholeness within. In alchemy, the sacred marriage of masculine and feminine forces, solar and lunar, creates a new force that is greater than the sum of its parts. This is true in relationships and it's also true within ourselves.

I love this next practice—it's such a beautiful way to step into a place of balance and self-honoring. You're going to write out your vows between your inner masculine and feminine. It's the same idea as the traditional wedding vows you would see between two people, but you are going to do this for yourself. See these vows as commitments to yourself, a way of choosing yourself fully and a declaration of coming into full harmony within. You want to start broad, but also try to get specific and practical. For example, if one of your vows from your masculine to your feminine is to be present and provide; list out what this actually looks like. Maybe it's creating space every day, 30 minutes in silence and presence, to listen to the deep inner world of your feminine emotions. To provide, he will make sure she is always living in a beautiful home, eating nourishing healthy foods and has an abundance of money in the bank. Then you can do the same from your inner feminine to masculine. This could include committing to nurturing your masculine side, through acts such as cooking nourishing meals for this part of you, or devoting time to awaken eros and love through self-pleasure practices.

Now, take out your journal and write the following:

- Your vows or commitments from your inner masculine to your inner feminine
- Your vows or commitments from your inner feminine to your inner masculine

To seal this inner union you can buy a ring as a symbol of this union, create a sacred space for yourself and speak these vows out loud and place the ring on your marriage finger to seal it in. You can wear the ring or you can keep the ring as a symbol on your altar at home. It's nice to invite someone you love and trust to witness these vows, like you would invite loved ones to a wedding. Get as creative as you can. Go all out—this is your inner wedding day, after all! And don't forget to consummate your inner union! That's what we're going to dive into in our next code, which is all about how a Sex Priestess self-sources her sexual energy—her eros.

CODE 4:

SELF-SOURCED EROS

Now that you've created a more loving and harmonious relationship between your inner masculine and feminine, you're ready to get to the juicy stuff: tapping into your own well of infinite love, pleasure and fulfillment.

Code 4 is all about reclaiming all parts of your sexuality as a woman and releasing those parts that are still looking for fulfillment, pleasure and love in outside sources (partners, lovers, male attention, success, validation, or any other external source). Here, we'll explore how to start sourcing from within. This is such a powerful code of the Sex Priestess, and one that requires you to learn and unlearn old behaviours and patterns so that you can truly be the source of your own *eros*. Psychoanalysts define eros as the life instinct, based on the libido, sublimated desires beyond lust and therefore cultivation of self-preservation. When I use the term eros, I am referring to the wellspring of sexual energy available inside of us that is an accumulation of desires, connected to our libido, or life force and indeed does preserve ones vital most essential force within. Most people are not sourcing this vital energy from within—instead, they're looking to find it outside of themselves, which results in a loss of personal power and a disconnection from the source of one's own sexuality and vitality. This code is about learning how to quit giving away our power and to take it back into our own hands, once and for all.

Let's start by exploring this concept of "self-sourcing." What does this even mean? We are energetic beings, and we are fed energetically by two separate planes of existence. The first is the vertical plane, which is the energetic dimension that consists of pure life force energy, prana or kundalini. The second is the horizontal plane, which is the physical dimension and the energy sources found on this earthly plane, such as food, water, and the life force of other humans. The first plane moves up and down through our being, and the second plane moves from the sides. Most people are disconnected from the vertical plane of existence, from the source of pure energy within and around us. Instead, they live by sourcing their energy purely from the horizontal plane. That means getting the energy fix you need from things like sugar, caffeine, carbs, other people's energy, or anything that gives you a dopamine hit. It can be manifested in overeating, overconsuming, having sex with others purely to take from the other, and energetically vampiring one another (you might be suprised how much people do this as a way to get the energy they need and crave, without being aware that they are doing it). Energetic vampiring is a term used to describe people who sometimes intentionally, but mostly unconsciously, drain your emotional energy. We all know what it's like to interact with an energy vampire. They feed on your attention; your willingness to listen and care for them, leaving you exhausted and overwhelmed. I like to believe this is not something people are doing consciously, most of the time. It's more of an unconscious survival mechanism, and a byproduct of a lack of self-love. When we're not giving ourselves what we need and desire, we are forced to look for it elsewhere. Notice when you feel sad, "off," or like you need to take a nap after being around someone, as this is a clear indicator that you experienced a loss of energy in the interaction.

An integral part of the process of waking up to your true power is switching from sourcing your energy on the horizontal plane to sourcing your energy on the vertical plane, from the Source of life itself. This is what yoga and tantra helps us with. We learn to source our energy from the Source within, so we don't have to rely so much on physical matter and other people for energy. This is why so many advanced yogis and tantrikas can eat very minimally and barely sleep, and they're thriving. At the most advanced level, a yogi can survive on the breath alone. This is because they are being fed from pure Source pranic energy, which is infinite and abundant.

When it comes to sexuality in particular, it's important to look at whether you are sourcing from the vertical or the horizontal plane. When we connect to the vertical plane and allow it to nourish us, we are practicing self-sourcing. But what happens when we are sourcing ourselves sexually from the horizontal plane? Sexuality is one of the biggest places where most people source from the horizontal plane, drawing from the energy of other people to meet their own needs. Why do we attempt to source energy off of others through sexual exchange? Because we have forgotten our true power and sovereignty. We have forgotten how to love ourselves. We don't know how to fill our own cup. We're disconnected from our own sexual energy and ability to experience pleasure and bliss naturally, on our own. This is one of the greatest distortions around our sexuality: we use it as an energy exchange, devoid of love and sacredness. But once we start learning how to self-regulate, self-source and self-love, we can come to another from a place of overflow and abundance. Then, we are able to share in what this sacred act is truly for: co-creation, alchemy and love. There are two sides to this equation: 1) Being fully connected to your own inner source of sexual energy and pleasure; and 2) Being able to share and further increase your energy through healthy and conscious sexual exchange.

For many years, I struggled to be self-sourced. Still processing the sexual violation from my childhood, I struggled to love myself and recognize (let alone meet) my own needs. This is what happens when you've experienced sexual abuse or violation in any form: a complete dissolution and blurriness of physical and sexual boundaries. This is due to the fact you had your boundaries so violated at an age where you didn't know how to express your "no"—so it becomes very difficult to distinguish your "yes" and "no" later in life. When sexual abuse has occured, there is also often a seeking of love and attention underneath it. What that means is that a lot of women who have experienced this kind of violation go down the path of promiscuity as a way of seeking the love and affection from men that was so absent in their previous sexual experiences.

This was certainly the case for me, and I spent most of my early 20s going from lover to lover. I remember not being able to go a month without a lover. It was like being thirsty in the desert; I had this constant thirst that never got quenched. I longed for love and affection so badly, and I could only find it through having sex with man after man, sourcing my energy from the horizontal plane, from each of the men I was with. I had no idea how to feel turned on or satisfy myself if I wasn't having sex with someone. During this time I also had a couple of two-year-long relationships, so it wasn't just casual sex nonstop. But in my single times, I did have a kind of addiction to constantly having someone I was entertaining with sex. Ultimately it didn't bring me any satisfaction because the gaping hole inside me was still there after each encounter. It was like a temporary hit of a drug that would last for a few hours after each sexual encounter and then leave me back in a place of emptiness and longing. This is what happens when we grasp for anything outside of ourselves. We never find the satisfaction we're looking for. When we source our eros from the outside, we never feel the fullness of our own life force, which is what we're actually looking for. To do that—which is to experience the true fullness, pleasure and joy of who we truly are—we must learn to source our sense of love, validation and especially our pleasure from within. Everything we need already exists inside of us; we just need to believe it and learn to access it.

This can be difficult in a world full of illusion that is always demanding attention on things outside. But those who dare to look within will find all the love, fulfillment and pleasure one could ever dream of—completely beyond what the outside illusionary world can give you. With our attention rooted inside of ourselves, we can begin sourcing our vital energy from the vertical plane, which is what I call self-sourcing.

The Unhealthy/Healthy Seductress Archetype

I want to first speak about the seductress archetype, which can play a big role here. Our seductress energy is such a powerful force. It's a natural part of the feminine allure. Feminine energy is by nature seductive. It's the magnetic force by which a woman allures and draws what she wants towards herself. A woman's natural energy is not going out and getting; it is magnetizing and receiving. However, when a woman is not self-sourcing is when she begins to fall into the unhealthy seductress archetype, or the shadow seductress. This is what I was embodying for most of my 20s. The shadow seductress uses her eros and feminine allure to draw in and seduce, but for the purpose of self-validation as opposed to actual love or connection. She needs others to validate her and will seduce and use that energy for self-serving or manipulation purposes. Each energy hit is only temporary and she will soon find herself prowling again to receive the attention and validation that she is still craving.

The other side to this is the healthy seductress, who is self-sourcing her own eros and therefore has an overflow of energy. She radiates her feminine energy, which is also magnetic, but it's rooted in a different frequency. She doesn't need others to validate her. Instead, she self-validates and self-loves. She radiates her feminine beauty and magnetism, which draws in others who are also of a similar or complementary frequency—those who are also self-sourced. There is no manipulation or self-service behind her intention, but rather service to a higher force beyond her egoic need for validation. This is the evolution of the seductress: moving from self-loathing to self-love and self-sourcing. One of the most powerful allies on my own journey towards self-sourcing was the Jade Egg, which came to me in my late 20s and was the key to learning how to self-source, love myself more deeply, refine and circulate my sexual energy and simply radiate it, rather than using it for validation. This magical little egg came to me when I had had enough of placing my ability to feel turned on and sexy in the hands of the next guy that came my way. I wanted to feel fully juicy and abundant and blissed-out on my own terms. I decided to learn how to feel this for myself, with myself.

The Jade Egg

The Jade Egg is a powerful ancient tantric practice with its origins in the Taoist tradition. Like tantra, Taoism uses sexual energy as a force for healing and spiritual awakening. It dates back over 5,000 years to ancient China, where the empresses and concubines of the Royal Palace of China used eggs carved out of jade to access their sexual power. It was believed that health, beauty, happiness and vitality could all be achieved through a strong and healthy yoni. To support the health of the yoni, they used jade, which was considered the most precious stone for its miraculous healing and magical properties. The practice was reserved only for the select royalty and not common knowledge to the general public, for these empresses and concubines knew that awakening the full power of one's sexual energy came with much responsibility. The women knew when their vaginas were activated and toned, they would experience better orgasms, more vitality because of the redirection of their sexual energy beyond the primal centres and up into creative centres and higher states of consciousness and love. They also knew they would be able to support the emperor to achieve better orgasms, as well as themselves, through being deeply rooted to their own pleasure capacity with a toned and healed vagina. The Jade Egg is now a widespread practice across the world, popularized by celebrities and influencers. But the roots of the practice remain just as strong as ever before. I think it says a lot about the times we're living in that a practice that was kept secret for the elites to master their sexual energy is now common practice for everyday people—which is a good thing, if you know how to use it correctly.

There's a saying about tantra, *It's like giving dynamite to a child*. This is likely why the ancient tantriks kept these powerful practices secret, because once you wake up the dragon (so to speak), you have to be able to ride it, so it doesn't blow fire on you. This is symbolic of our sexuality. It's one thing to learn how to awaken it, but then it is about learning how to manage this powerful force within. The Jade Egg has been such a powerful tool for myself and many of my clients in refining their sexual energy and learning how to channel it into higher states of consciousness, beyond lust and primal sexual urges.

You may doubt its power, but you really need to try it for yourself to know what I'm talking about. I truly believe the jade egg is the sex preistess's greatest ally. It has been such a gift along my own journey and that of many of my students. The egg itself is a semi-precious stone that carries healing properties for physical, mental, emotional and spiritual balance, particularly for purifying, detoxing and cleansing the vital fluids in the body. This tiny crystal egg is inserted inside the vagina and combined with a variety of breathing practices and physical postures, which also helps tone the lower abdomen and strengthen the pelvic floor muscles. When the pelvic floor muscles are toned and strong, they serve as a floor for all our vital organs and an energetic seal for our life force. Instead of the life force naturally flowing downward from the navel, and then leaking out through the root chakra, when your pelvic floor muscles are toned, this vital energy starts to get redirected upwards and throughout the body. The ancient Taoist tantrikas knew this and considered it the key to youthfulness and vitality. When these muscles are strong, they prevent leakage of our vital life force and sexual energy and help us harness this energy for creative and healing purposes.

The jade egg practice was first introduced to me by a sister of mine who now owns a large yoni crystal company in Australia. She gifted me my first jade egg and I began by just exploring it intuitively for a couple years. It wasn't until a few years later that I was taught some of the powerful jade egg foundational practices through the work of Mantak Chia and a beautiful woman named Halo Sorenko, who holds jade egg courses through her school Shakti Temple Arts, which is listed in the appendix at the end of the book. The first couple years where I was intuitively working with the egg was very powerful. I felt as though my body was teaching me how to develop my own relationship and practice with it. This was very important for me to do before getting formal training because I learned that my body had some kind of memory of what to do with it. I always encourage my students to do the same: buy an egg and let your intuition and body guide you through the process. Then, if you want to get more formal training, you can go from there. I teach the jade egg basic practice as part of all of my online courses, such as The Creatress and Pleasure Principles. You can also find other resources from my mentors mentioned in the appendix at the end of the book.

Working with this practice, I began to tangibly experience a gradual releasing of my need to look outside of myself for love, attention and validation. I could actually feel and experience my life force and eros circulating throughout my body, which was something I had never fully felt before. I began to feel so much more connected to my body, and also to learn how to call my energy back to my center from all the places where I had been unconsciously leaking it out. At the time, I was healing from a breakup and I decided that I needed to go deep into my sexual sovereignty and break this pattern of the unhealthy seductress once and for all. During this 18-month period of being single, I practiced the jade egg regularly and experienced so many benefits: more energy, more self-love, and a deeper connection to the sacredness of my sexuality. I even witnessed reverse aging! Your own life force and sexual energy is the most potent anti-aging remedy you will ever find out there—as the ancient tantriks knew. When your life force is circulating and not leaking, you get that natural glow. This practice is truly remarkable. Whenever women ask me where to begin with learning tantra, I always suggest starting with the jade egg practice as an embodied experience of connecting to your most vital energy and learning how to work with it, channel it and circulate it throughout your body.

The jade egg practice is also very powerful for supporting women to heal sexual trauma in a safe and sacred way. When a woman has experienced any form of sexual violation or abuse—or even simply being entered without presence and awareness—this trapped energy and tension is stored in her vagina. In order to release the trapped energy, tension and associated unprocessed emotions, we must massage the tissue of the vaginal canal to trigger a physical and energetic release. Of course, you can't exactly get this kind of massage when you go for a regular massage, nor would this be a healing experience! There needs to be a level of safety and trust in order for a woman to open and heal the tension in the first place. This is where the jade egg comes in. It's a practice you can do yourself, and it's very empowering in that respect. This includes deep massaging techniques of sliding the egg in and out of the vagina canal while breathing, releasing and training the nervous system to relax. It's also important to invite the egg inside instead of just pushing it in when the vagina isn't prepared to open. The massaging of the internal vaginal walls helps release any tension and stuck emotions that may be residing there from the original sexual trauma incident. You can find a list of the best quality Jade Eggs at my resource page as mentioned in the appendix at the end of the book.

Basic Jade Egg Practice

Here's a basic beginner practice you can try to get started with the jade egg. The goal is to introduce you to the egg and to your pelvic floor muscles. At the same time, it gently gives you a full internal massage of the yoni walls, supporting the release of stuck energy and emotions. You want to make sure you have a drilled egg with the string attached already.

1. Hold the egg and place into it your intention for your practice
2. Begin with a deeply nourishing breast massage, drawing circles around your breasts, first with your open palms, and then with the tips of your fingers
3. Slide your egg over your womb and begin to massage your womb with the egg, infusing your intention from the egg into the womb with this first introduction
4. Massage the outer yoni lips with the egg.
5. Next, place the wide side of the egg at the entrance of your yoni opening, hold it here by the string and breathe. Slowly rotate your hips back and forward as you inhale invite in the egg. Slowly "sip" in the egg over 10-20 breaths.
6. Once inserted, take the string and start to slide the egg down towards the yoni entrance, as you inhale 'suck' it back up inside of you, using your yoni muscles to squeeze it inside, then exhale using your hand on the string gently pull the egg towards the yoni entrance, then repeat inhale and "suck" the egg back inside of you, exhale with the support of your hand on the string pull the egg downwards. Continue this for 22 rounds.

7. Pause and allow any emotions to arise.
8. Slowly, over 10-20 breaths, remove the egg from inside of you.
9. Journal about your experience.

Self-pleasure, Self-love, Self-sourcing

After the jade egg practice, the next practice in self-sourcing is developing a self-pleasure practice. Self-pleasure is a form of self-love, and self-love is a form of self-sourcing. How can we love anyone else if we don't love ourselves? And how are we meant to pleasure anyone else or even know what we desire if we don't know how to pleasure ourselves? You might be surprised how many women I work with have no self-pleasure practice or have never even touched themselves. As I shared, my self-pleasure practice began very young. I just assumed this is what everyone did. It wasn't until I reached high school that I asked my friends if they masturbated, and 70% of them said no and were repulsed by the idea. I thought there might be something wrong with me because of the fact that I started at six years old, but turns out I was perfectly fine. This eros energy running through us is so natural. As young children we are naturally curious about it. If we feel safe in our home environments and our bodies, we will naturally begin to explore it at a young age. To *not* feel comfortable to explore this powerful energy in an innocent and curious way is actually what many people come to me to work with as adults. They are seeking out my support to learn how to connect to their bodies and pleasure as adult women. It is truly a beautiful reclamation.

The problem starts with the fact that many women don't feel worthy of pleasure. My own journey with pleasure, too, was up and down. It was such a source of joy to me as a young girl, and then when I experienced a sexual trauma at seven years old, I came to associate pleasure with shame. During these formative years before the age of ten, but especially before the age of six years old, everything we experience has a huge impact on our lifelong core belief systems. If we've experienced any negative or traumatic early sexual experiences, or have been taught distorted beliefs around sex (such as that it's sinful or dirty), this can create neural pathways in the brain that associate pleasure with pain, shame, guilt and even powerlessness. This is not limited to sex but can include any form of pleasure in life. Each time I would enjoy self-pleasure, afterwards there would be a dark cloud of guilt and shame that would follow. This manifested in all sorts of ways, including associating guilt and shame with other pleasures of life, like food. I would enjoy delicious foods and then feel a sense of shame and guilt to follow. This became the root cause of the eating disorder I suffered from as a teenager. I started to feel shame in my body, the source of my feminine essence, stemming from the sexual experience I had as a seven-year-old. Whenever a woman comes to me with an eating disorder, I always go back to her history with her sexuality. Our relationship to our sexuality and body is so intertwined. Healing starts with clearing out any residual stagnant emotions from the body itself through self-pleasure sessions. This becomes the gateway to open up to more pleasure and orgasmic energy.

Barriers to Pleasure: Unprocessed Trauma

Connecting to our pleasure bodies is so important as women. This is what connects us to the body itself and to the orgasmic frequency. The Orgasmic Frequency is essentially another name for life force or eros that powers everything in nature, and that is running through all plants, animals and living beings that inhabit this planet. It is not about becoming a hedonist. For many women who have experienced some level of sexual trauma or shut down, there is a disconnection from the body that occurs, causing pain or numbness in the genitals themselves. This can manifest as a tense vagina, pain or numbness during lovemaking, a lack of desire, heavy periods, and chronic period pain. These are all ways your body is signaling that there is something deeper to address beneath the physical pain. The physical pain is just the body's way of trying to communicate deeper unconscious emotion associated with a traumatic experience.

It's not just a handful of people who experience this. There are so many people on the planet walking around in a state of freeze, which is a common trauma response which creates a sense of numbness. When I speak about sexual trauma, the spectrum can vary from hard trauma such as rape to a softer trauma, like being entered forcefully or without full presence from a sexual partner (even a boyfriend). It can also include energetic enmeshment from a parent who projects sexual energy onto their child. The softer trauma is one of the most underestimated sexual traumas there is. Think about when you were younger and sexually active without half the awareness you have now. Remember all those times you had one-night stands with random guys who were clearly not entering you with the love, devotion and presence that you know you deserve. Each time this happens to a woman, her body signals to her brain *I am not safe*, and a layer of armor starts to build. This starts energetically and then becomes a physical armor with a tightening of the muscles inside the vaginal canal itself, contractions in the womb, and energetic layers of protection over the heart. For heavy trauma, the severity of this armoring goes deeper, manifesting in severe pain, numbness and disassociation. Numbness in either the emotional and or physical body is almost always a result of some level of psychological, emotional or physical trauma.

How Sexual Trauma Causes Physical & Emotional Shutdown

When we have experienced any level of trauma, often the intensity of the emotion getting activated is way too much to process in that given moment, especially if we are a young child. It overwhelms the central nervous system, triggering a fight, flight or freeze response. The subconscious has a way of processing this so the conscious self can avoid feeling completely out of control. What happens is that the memory gets stored in the subconscious mind for us to deal with later when it is safe to do so. When the trauma occurs, the nervous system will respond with fight, flight or freeze. In this moment of overwhelm, the system gets stuck—this locks us into this state of being going forward in our life until we go back and fully process the trauma.

The unprocessed trauma can then manifest in all sorts of psychological and physical disorders. It's important to really understand the three trauma responses so that we can identify how our body might be holding onto an old experience of sexual trauma: *Flight* is when the body releases stress hormones to give the body the energy to physically flee the situation. *Fight* is when the person develops strong feelings of anger or rage and sometimes acts on these feelings when triggered in the original trauma. *Freeze* is the numbness response so the person will numb out and also feel completely dissociated, cold and frozen emotionally. This happens when the trauma is too much the person dissociates and leaves their body altogether, blacking out or just completely vacating the physical body. Psychologists call this dissociation and shamans call it "soul loss"—what both terms are expressing is that a part of the self, or the soul, leaves the body in the moment of traumatic overwhelm. When working with sexual trauma, we want to focus on repairing the nervous system and allowing the woman to return to a state of safety in her physical body. This gives her a chance to feel whatever emotions are there underneath the frozen or numb sensations in the vagina itself.

When sexual trauma has occured, the two most important things for healing are:

1. Safety (feeling safe again in your own body)
2. Accessing to your "no" & asserting strong boundaries

This is why working with practices such as the jade egg and the self-pleasure guided practices later in this chapter are so effective, because YOU are in control of your healing. YOU are taking back your own capacity for pleasure from the people and experiences earlier in life that may have robbed you of it. You don't have to wait around for someone else to establish a level of trust that makes you feel safe to surrender. This is why I always start with facilitating these *self-led* practices with women who have experienced any level of sexual trauma, from the softest to the most hardcore. This allows the woman to let go. Through creating a sense of safety of her nervous system by allowing her to experience pleasure in a way that feels nourishing to her, she begins to access some of the emotions underneath the pain or discomfort inside the vagina itself. Once she is able to feel the emotions that were too difficult to process at the time of the original traumatic incident, they are able to then alchemize and leave the body. As we've discussed, every emotion just wants to be felt and expressed. That is what its entire purpose is. Our emotions will not leave us, no matter how many years or decades have gone by, until we do this. Once these emotions literally leave the body, this is what opens us up to finally be able to feel again, including pleasure available. But in order to feel the pleasure, she must be willing to feel what is in the way. On an energetic level, these unprocessed emotions and traumas are blocking her from being a clear, receptive channel for source energy, life force and the orgasmic frequency to flow through. When you address the trauma and clear up the channel, the pleasure actually comes quite naturally and easily.

Pleasure Pathways

Let's take a look at the other side of the spectrum: pleasure pathways. One of the key ways to move from sexual trauma to liberation is by redefining pleasure altogether. Pleasure is often associated with sex, but, of course, pleasure expands far beyond the bedroom. On the journey to fully embodying the sex priestess, it's so important to cultivate more pleasure in all its expressions and to open up new neural pathways of pleasure. Some of these other pathways are through the five senses: taste and delicious foods, smell and luscious scents, sounds and beautiful music or frequencies, touch and non-sexual touch like a foot massage or beautiful fabrics, sight and beautiful art and scenery. Anything that ignites your senses can become a potent source of pleasure. To begin opening up to new pleasure pathways we can first start by arousing the five senses in our environment with pleasurable inputs. What this is doing is resensitizing you and connecting you back to the pleasure portals that are your senses.

Experiencing pleasure invites you deeper into the present moment, through the senses and into the body. When you are more deeply connected to your body, you can then feel what is true to be felt and alchemised, to allow for more pleasure to arise. Pleasure in itself is also a very healing state that relaxes the nervous system, quiets the mind and releases tension—the more authentic, healthy pleasure we experience in our lives (as opposed to artificial pleasure from substances or sourcing from the horizontal plane), the healthier we are on every level.

When you expand the pleasure capacity in your body, your entire life expands. Often we limit ourselves to our "go-to" pleasure pathways, the things that we know "work." For example, in sex you may know certain positions guarantee your peak orgasm, which is great—but that can limit you, because you don't know what you don't know. There's so much that lies in the unknown, outside the familiar. When it comes to expanding the pleasure pathways in the body, we often need to be pushed outside of our comfort zone, beyond what is familiar and what we know "works." It often comes down to letting go of control, surrendering and allowing another to take the lead—someone you deeply trust, whether that be a partner or a guide. Essentially, for a woman to truly let go and surrender into pleasure, she needs to feel safe and she needs to have a relaxed nervous system. There needs to be as much openness as possible and the least amount of resistance in her entire physical vessel. In that letting go of control and opening to something new (not just sticking to your old faithfuls), you can be initiated into a whole new pleasure pathway. And when you experience a new pleasure pathway, new neural pathways are created in your brain. This is like a divine pattern interruption, shaking things up on a physical, cellular level and opening you up to new fresh perspectives in all aspects of life. Old rigid ways of being and thinking now become fluid, and fresh creativity and inspiration emerges through you. This is why the keys to your empowerment do not dwell in textbooks. They are in your very body waiting to be unlocked.

Opening to Pleasure: The Heart and Emotional Penetration

Before we explore self-pleasure practices through the yoni, it's important to begin by acknowledging the heart space first. The gateway to a woman's pleasure and fully expressed eros is through her heart. When we look at the biological makeup of women, we can see that a woman's genitals are receptive and her heart is penetrative, literally her breasts point out and give life to her child. The opposite is true for a man. His genitals penetrate the world and he does not have breasts that produce life-giving milk. So a woman receives through her yoni and gives through her heart. Because of this she needs her heart to be penetrated first—or what I like to call emotional penetration—before she opens up sexually. The opposite is true for a man, whose heart actually opens after his sexual energy opens. This is why a woman's sexuality is like water and a man's is like fire. Women need so much more time to open up and "boil" like water. On average, a woman reaches orgasm after about 40 minutes of foreplay, whereas a man can reach orgasm within three to five minutes. The deeper the emotional bond with a beloved, the deeper the female orgasm and opening of the feminine *eros*.

All women desire to be penetrated at the heart space before being penetrated sexually. What this looks and feels like is time to establish and build trust, and time for a woman to truly feel seen and heard by the man. If we haven't had an embodied experience of honoring our *own* heart's needs first, then it is very difficult for us to lead a man to our heart space. One of the most powerful ways to activate the heart center first is through sacred self-breast massage. Every day after your morning shower, or before bed, spend some time massaging your breasts. This immediately draws your attention to your physical breasts and thus the energetic heart.

Another important way of honoring your heart's needs is to ask yourself what your core needs in a relationship are. What you need to feel safe with your partner in order to open up sexually? When you can really feel within yourself what it feels like to tend to your own heart first, you can then bring that experience to your encounters with men, inviting them to your heart space first. You don't give out sex straight off the bat before establishing any sort of emotional penetration. As women, I believe that the sex should always get better and better for this reason. We are so much more emotionally driven, so the deeper the emotional bond and trust (which takes time to build), the better the orgasms get over the duration of a longer-term relationship.

At the end of the day, we can only meet others to the degree that we have met ourselves. If we want intimacy, trust and devotion in a partnership, we must become intimate with ourselves, learn to trust ourselves, and be completely devoted to ourselves. The intimacy we long for with another becomes available to us once we have become intimate with ourselves. There are many ways to cultivate this, but the act of making love to yourself is the ultimate act of intimacy and devotion to yourself. When you feel this on an embodied level, and know yourself in this intimate way, you can invite your lover into this space with you. The level of pleasure you can experience with your partner depends on the level of pleasure you have cultivated within yourself, first and foremost.

Yoni De-armoring Practice

With an open heart and honoring of our emotional needs, we can begin the deeper work with the yoni. In addition to the jade egg, there's one particular modality I recommend that was critical in my own journey of healing my sexual trauma at the deepest embodied level. I always use this practice when I guide clients through a healing self-pleasure session focusing on releasing sexual trauma and associated emotions. The practice is called *yoni de-armoring*, also known as yoni mapping or yoni reflexology. It's the foundation of a basic tantric yoni massage that a tantric practitioner or sexuality bodyworker would perform on a woman. However, because my work is about empowering women to be in control and feel 100% safe through this process, I've modified this to be a *self*-yoni massage. Feeling safe is the absolute foundation of healing sexual trauma. As I described earlier, one of the most common trauma responses is the freeze response, which ends up manifesting as a numbness inside the woman's vagina, blocking her from feeling any pleasure. Depending on the severity of the trauma, if it was soft or hardcore trauma, there can be different level of physical "armor" literally built up inside the vagina canal. A number of women have shared with me that they feel so much tightness and pain in their vagina, as if it is sealed over and does not want anything to enter. This is usually a huge sign of unresolved sexual trauma ranging from being entered before you were ready to full-blown rape.

Every experience is valid and worthy of attention and healing, so please, do not underestimate the impact of seemingly soft traumas. Even feeling unsafe in a man's presence can create a subtle contraction and tension in your yoni and womb. As women, we are such receptive and sensitive beings. By our very nature as women, we are always receiving masculine penetration— physically, emotionally, psychologically and energetically. Every time this penetration makes us feel unsafe, and the emotion is too intense to face, it will manifest as a layer of energetic armor inside the vagina canal, and even on the external vagina. We do this naturally and unconsciously to protect ourselves from being entered by someone who feels threatening on some level. The point of yoni de-armoring is to massage the yoni internally with simple acupressure techniques and the help of a yoni wand (see appendix to purchase recommended yoni wands). This releases any of the stuck energy and associated emotions underneath the numbness or hardness inside the yoni. Just like you would receive a massage on your body, when certain muscles are poked and prodded, pain may arise. Underneath the physical pain or tension is usually an emotion that is trapped there. The exact same thing is happening inside a woman's vagina. This practice helps release the armor and allow the woman to safely access the trapped emotions that simply want to be felt and seen.

Sex Priestess

And to be clear, you don't necessarily have to have experienced trauma to participate in this practice. This practice can be done simply as a beautiful internal yoni massage to deepen your capacity for pleasure, and as a way to access what is going on for you. Your yoni is always the gatekeeper of truth, of what is true on the deepest embodied level. So whatever emotions arise from this practice are usually a great indicator of what is going on for you and what needs to be addressed. I often say that my yoni is my oracle, and I believe this to be true for most women. The body does not lie.

The technique itself is quite simple:

1. Begin your practice with a breast massage, to draw the attention to the heart space before entering the vagina.
2. Massage the outer vagina with some coconut oil, taking your time to release any tension stored in the yoni lips.
3. Hold the yoni wand's smaller tip at the entrance of your yoni, and allow your yoni to 'invite' in the wand, only inserting it once you feel ready to receive it. You can move your hips in a sliding motion combined with slow breathing to help open the pelvis and hips in order to invite in the yoni wand inside of you. (This technique, which I also use in the jade egg practice, is one of the most healing parts of the practice as it requires your brain and body to feel safe to be entered as YOU say yes and welcome in penetration. This helps heal all those times you may have been entered without permission or prematurely.)
4. Once the wand is inside of you, hold it here for a few moments and breathe, allowing the emotions to arise.
5. Take the tip of the wand and, as if you are pressing the numbers around a clock, you are going to start at 12 o'clock and apply some light pressure here inside your vagina, just over the G-spot. From here, taking your

time, make your way around the entire 'clock,' moving slightly to the right to 1 o'clock, 2 o'clock, 3 o'clock, until you make your way back to the start—a full circle. You want to make sure you spend as much time on each point as needed, inhale and then as you exhale apply some pressure on each point and apply a gentle massage, and allow any emotions and sensations to arise. Continue in that spot until the energy dissipates and feels neutral.

Orgasm & the Feminine Archetypes

In my own sexual healing journey, and also with the women I work with, I began working with different feminine archetypes and their links with different parts of the body, and specifically, different types of orgasm. At the start of my feminine embodiment journey, I worked with archetypes as a way to access deeper layers of the unconscious mind. It was a profound practice for me and for my students. What I started to realize was that these archetypes live in certain places inside our female body—and again, no theory or intellectual understanding could help us liberate and truly embody these archetypes. The work must be done through the body.

I found that the maiden archetype lives in our clitoris, which embodies innocence, exploration and play. The wild woman lives in our G-spot, which embodies the fullest unleashing of our messy wildness. The mystic lives in our cervix, as the literal bridge between the worlds. Each has its own corresponding orgasm—heart, clitoris, G-spot and cervical. This has been such a powerful exploration into opening up new pleasure pathways through bringing awareness to each of these places within the feminine psyche and erotic body.

Clitoris and the Maiden Archetype

The first orgasm is the clitoris, which is linked to the maiden archetype. This is where we are first met in order to create safety. Our maiden is linked to our erotic innocence and holds the gateway to this longing for safety as the foundation of surrendering to a worthy masculine partner. The clitoris is typically the first place we explore when our sexuality begins blossoming, and it holds that innocent maiden energy as we age and mature. Through stimulating our clitoris, where we hold this archetype in the body, we can access and heal the wounds of our inner maiden. If we do not honor our maiden archetype—which invites a partner to meet us at the heart space first—then we will never feel the full body "yes" to that partner. The maiden commonly gets expressed in our younger years pre-pubescent and teenage years, where we begin exploring ourselves and this new found connection to our sexuality. But sadly, the maiden within most of us has been heavily suppressed due to the culture we live in, where sexual abuse is so common and women are over-sexualised from such a young age, and often feel forced to grow up too quickly. We lose our sense of feminine innocence and purity very early on. The maiden is the part of us deeply connected to our erotic innocence and has full trust in love, for she hasn't yet been hurt and become jaded. Because of this, she is radiant.

My maiden years began at the age of five or six, when I started exploring my own sexuality and pleasure. And not long after, that erotic innocence and full trust in love was stripped from me after the sexual abuse occurred. Ironically, the violation was him touching my clitoris, this most pleasurable place that I found and loved; and yet now which was holding so much shame. My purity and erotic innocence now felt shut down and suppressed. Later in my life, whenever I would self-pleasure with my clitoris, I would feel shame shortly afterwards. I later reclaimed this part of myself by consciously self-pleasuring with a sole focus on the clitoris, allowing myself to fully enjoy the pleasure, free of guilt and shame. I reclaimed my maiden and erotic innocence through this process.

Many women are not guided properly through their maiden initiation years, and they experience having their erotic innocence stripped of them. So many young girls are peer pressured into having sex so young, before they are psychologically ready, bypassing their sense of self-worth and self-love. With all the social media influence now, I cannot even imagine how difficult it must be for young girls growing up with all the pressures, unrealistic beauty standards, over-sexualisation, instagram filters, plastic surgery and peer pressure. It is a real cultural sickness and a major issue we need to face collectively.

The most powerful thing for creating a healthy maiden archetype in our psychological makeup isn't what you might think. When a young girl is first exploring her sexuality, what anchors a healthy imprint of her sexuality being connected to her heart—as well as a visceral sense of safety in her body—is the presence of her father in his fullest healthy masculine unconditional love frequency.

When young girls begin exploring their sexuality at home, the father may accidentally witness this—or even just feel into her blossoming sexual energy—and feel extremely uncomfortable and then reject her or shame her for her explorations. Later in her teenage years, when she starts developing breasts and womanly curves, he may shame her subtly with comments like *you can't go out wearing that* or *put on more clothes*—all giving her the impression that her natural feminine eros is not okay. She feels that she is being rejected by the one man whose acceptance she most longs for. Or, if the father is not getting his own sexual needs met by his wife, he may unconsciously project his frustrated sexual desire onto his young daughter, feeling drawn to her blossoming sexual energy, and the associated shame that comes with that is then projected onto the daughter as well. The daughter begins to feel extremely uncomfortable and unsafe in her maiden, and often shuts down her sexuality and feminine nature to protect herself.

In both cases, she is being robbed of the unconditional love from the father that she needs and craves. Her first imprint is being formed of rejection (or violation) from the father, just for being in her natural essence and her erotic innocence. This then fragments her from the father, from the masculine, which becomes a pattern that gets etched in her psyche and clitoris. What a young girl truly needs in this moment is the presence of the father as he witnesses her, without judgment or shame or unconscious attraction and desire. He doesn't need to talk about it with her, but there needs to be a level of understanding and maturity within the father to be able to simply witness, without judgment, his daughter in her blossoming maiden expression. I am not saying that he should watch her self-pleasure. The idea is that if he were to witness her, or even if he just feels the energy of her sexuality, he does not react by demonizing her. He simply witnesses without judgment and keeps loving her. This could look as simple as saying to her, when she comes downstairs in her dress and makeup, *You look beautiful darling, your father loves you*. If this is her experience, she will form a first healthy imprint that her sexuality blossoming in her body is safe. She will know that it is safe in her body, the masculine accepts her, and through the father's love, she will link sexuality with love. This is the core foundation of a woman's healthy sexuality later in life. When she feels this, she will respect her body and her sexuality and remain connected to her heart. In order to respect a man and eventually open her body to him, she will have to feel the same level of love that she received from her father. She will become an adult woman with healthy self-worth.

The clitoris can be seen as the physical dwelling of the maiden archetype in the feminine body. Beyond the role of the father, if we haven't received the proper initiations or we have experienced any form of sexual abuse or violation in our maiden years, this pure pleasure portal embodying our erotic innocence starts to shut down. We start to distrust the masculine, we distrust love, we disconnect from play and pure pleasure, and we don't hold strong boundaries or self-worth when it comes to letting partners enter our body temple. The clitoris is also like the temple bell of the yoni temple itself, for it is on the external and can be stimulated without penetration. When our clitoris gets aroused we also become more ready to be penetrated. What is happening psychologically is that we need to feel our maiden is honored first before being entered. When we have a healthy maiden archetype we ask ourselves if we feel loved, respected and safe with this person before we allow them inside the temple. This sense of our own sacredness gets restored by reclaiming the maiden within through self-pleasure practice solely dedicated to the clitoris. To start this practice, the invitation is to set aside some time tonight to reconnect with this part of yourself. Make a playlist that feels sweet and gentle to get you in the mood. Begin with a breast massage to open the heart space, then slowly make your way to exploring, very curiously and innocently, massaging only the outer vagina, including the clitoris. To go deeper into this practice, you can find a guided version in my online self-pleasure course, Pleasure Principles (see resource link in appendix). After your practice, stay cozy in bed, grab your journal and take some time to make your way through the self-inquiry journal prompts below:

- If you could paint the picture of your inner maiden, who is she? What does she look like? What brings her joy and pleasure? Describe her...
- How did you express yourself in your maiden years?

- What makes you feel connected to the maiden aspect of yourself now?
- What does this maiden aspect of you desire most?
- What is your relationship to your clitoris and clitoral orgasm?
- What are some of the barriers that arise when you explore clitoral stimulation?
- Are there any strong memories and emotions that arise when you explore clitoral stimulation?
- What brings you the most pleasure?
- What does your maiden need in order to open up sexually to a partner?
- Ask your inner maiden: where and how can you bring more play into your life?

G-spot and the Wild Woman

The next orgasm and archetype is the G-spot orgasm and the wild woman. The wild woman is our connection to our true wild nature. She helps us express our boundaries, know our worth, express our needs and unlock our fullest creative expression and gifts to the world. She is that unbridled, fearless, shameless aspect of us that needs no permission or validation from outside of herself. She walks her own path, not caring what anybody thinks of her. This archetype is embodied in our G-spot, purely because this is where we experience what we know as female ejaculation or *amrita* ("nectar"). This very expression of the female body is wild and messy. It is a deeper orgasm, a more wild orgasm. Once we feel the maidens need for safety being honored, we can truly begin to explore more of this wild aspect of our sexuality. This can only happen when we feel safe and held in the relational container. The wild woman expresses on her own terms—she is not performing. There is no-performance based sexuality when she gets unlocked, for she strips away all those delusions of how she thinks she should be or what is conventionally seen as attractive. Rather, she shows up in her pure primal power, ruthless and raw, and she surrenders to however the erotic energy wants to move through her, with zero shame. This wild aspect of us usually gets suppressed and shut down when we have experienced some level of shame or guilt around our sexuality and self-expression. When we can heal this through G-spot self pleasure, we unlock the wild woman archetype and our wild aspect, which simultaneously unlocks our deepest creative gifts that are longing to be expressed. This is why the keys to unlocking your gifts do not dwell in textbooks or theories, but rather, again—in your body.

The G-spot itself is named after Ernst Grafenberg, a German gynecologist, whose 1940s research documented this sensitive region within the vagina of a woman. This in itself is crazy, that a male doctor has claimed his territory inside a woman's body and named this most wild embodied aspect of her after his name. So I like to refer to it as the G-oddess spot, as a way to take back the power women have over their own bodies. This is a very wild woman move. She does not adhere to ownership, especially over her body, for she is a wild, untamable creature. She belongs to no man. I invite you to also contemplate what you desire to name your G-spot. It could be something completely different, but the important thing is that it feels like you are taking back your power through this process.

I first met my inner wild woman when I decided to leave the bright lights and comforts of the city and venture into the wild hinterland of Byron Bay—a classic wild woman move. I found myself a cabin in the woods on a private farm where the closest neighbor was miles away. My little cabin was down deep on the property in the lush thick forest surrounded by cattle, magic mushrooms, a black cat and a python. The house was deep in the forest. It was pitch black, with no street lights as I made my way through windy roads of the hinterland to get home. This frightened me so much—driving at night in the dark, and then having to walk down this steep hill into my cabin, because I couldn't park down in the depths of the forest where my cabin was. For the first few months of living there, I made sure I was home before dark. This was so symbolic in itself. Coming from the bright lights of the city where I grew up, where everything is always lit up, it was very rare to see stars or have any pure darkness. Moving to a home surrounded by darkness, I saw this as a representation of what was happening in my psyche. I was facing the darkness, facing my fears. In the wild unknown of nature, I was meeting the wild outside and also within myself. After about three months I started to adjust to this new lifestyle, and slowly I became more and more feral as I attuned so deeply to the natural rhythms of the earth. I rarely wore shoes, I would pee outside, I would take baths under the moonlight in my outdoor bath, I made friends with the animals and began telepathically communicating with them. I didn't shave my legs or underarms and just truly went full feral wild woman. I began to feel safe to drive home at night and walk through the forest in the pitch dark. This was such an initiation.

I spent a year in this cabin in the deep hinterland of Byron Bay, becoming intimate with nature. One of the deepest initiations was meeting the python living under my stilted house. One beautiful afternoon I was meditating on my porch when I had a vision of a serpent in my third eye. At that moment I opened my eyes to see a three-meter python slithering past me, making its way back to its nest, which I soon discovered was underneath my bed, under the house. I froze, knowing that if I moved, it would get scared and potentially harm me. This encounter was nature's way of initiating me into facing deep survival fear. I truly believe that to fear the serpent is to fear our power, for the serpent is the life force kundalini energy fully unlocked within the human being. To be that close to this beautiful animal and then find out it had been sleeping essentially underneath me for the entire duration of my time there, was such a potent initiation into my wild woman through facing a deep collective fear. Entering the wild in any capacity will do this to you. It truly humbles us to the divine creator, and to the potency and force of the feminine and all of creation. The reflection of the wilderness invites us to meet the places where we have become overly domesticated in our comforts of a manufactured artificial life. It invites us to face our deepest fears, venomous animals, the pure darkness, the unpredictability and savage side of predators as they devour their prey. This wild part of us—the part that is not afraid of the dark, not scared to be messy, raw and unrestrained—needs to be fully unlocked if we are to truly come to peace with our humanity and embody our full power.

When the wild woman gets suppressed for too long, this starts to manifest in a woman's body through numbness in her yoni and specifically G-spot. What is usually underneath the numbness is an incredible amount of rage, anger or frustration. This is because when you try to lock up a wild creature for far too long, in an attempt to domesticate it—when a woman always does the "right thing," people-pleases, lives according to others' expectations of her—she becomes resentful. This resentment gets etched deeper and deeper in the psyche and manifests physically in the yoni. She becomes frustrated, passive aggressive and uptight. Her yoni is contracted and her gifts are frozen as she fears stepping out of the status quo and walking her own path outside of what is expected of her from society. She has not yet found her inner lioness roar.

To unlock the lioness, we go into the wildness within, through the body. The G-spot is where she dwells in the body, so any form of G-spot stimulation and guided self-pleasure practice, will support unlocking her creativity, melting down the frozen walls, and feeling whatever needs to be felt that is underneath that frozen numbness—especially rage. This practice can be very cathartic and healing. It involves using a yoni wand to deeply massage the internal walls of the yoni around the G-spot. I encourage you to explore this as an intuitive process.

Being witnessed and guided in accessing your rage can also support a healthy expression of the wild woman archetype. The most powerful rage release ritual I have found is somatic shaking, followed by pillow beating (this practice is detailed in Code 1 in the Emotional Alchemy section). To be able to release this intense emotion in a safe, contained way is incredibly healing, and allows you to reclaim that part of yourself that has been suppressed for far too long. It's the part of you that holds the memory of past-life persecution, the part that is angry at yourself for saying yes when you meant no, for allowing people to cross your boundaries, and for ultimately betraying yourself, living a life according to what others expect from you rather than what you truly want and who you truly are. This practice supports the reclamation of your sovereignty and power—that which only the wild woman can grant you full access to.

If you want to go deeper, I have a guided practice for G-spot stimulation and somatic release self-pleasure practice focused on de-armoring and massaging the G-spot (with either the finger or ideally a yoni wand). This guided practice can be found in my online self-pleasure course, Pleasure Principles (see resource link in appendix).

Of course, the best place to start is just by exploring intuitively on your own. Below are some self-inquiry journal prompts to begin this journey:

- If you could paint a picture of your inner wild woman, who is she? Describe her in detail...
- What does this wild aspect of you long for?

- How does your inner wild woman currently express herself? When do you feel most connected to this part of yourself?
- What happened that might have shut her down?
- What are some of your core boundaries? What is not welcome in your life/body?
- What is your relationship to G-spot orgasm?
- What are some of the blocks you are experiencing with G-spot orgasm?
- What aspects of your life feel out of alignment? Where do you feel "caged in"?
- What is holding you back from letting go of the parts that feel out of alignment?
- Ask your inner wild woman: what is longing to be birthed through you?
- Ask your inner wild woman: what gifts are waiting to be expressed?
- What would it look like to live completely free of others' judgments and perceptions of you?
- What are some of your erotic edges, kinks, desires and taboos?
- What do you need to let go of in order to trust fully in yourself?

Cervix and the Mystic

The third and final archetype we will explore is the mystic, who dwells in the cervix. The mystic holds our connection to a knowing beyond physical form and the limitations of time and space. She is the part of us who sees beyond the illusion of the mundane world, because she knows she is connected to something greater than the personal ego—a force that is the grand mystery of life itself. But she's not disconnected from the physical world and living in the clouds. Rather, she has mastered both the physical and non-physical dimensions of life, and knows how to dance between the two effortlessly, not getting attached to either one. She is connected to something much deeper and beyond what meets the eye, and therefore she can help you remember who you truly are beyond your limiting self-concepts. She helps you stay rooted in truth and divinity and not get so caught up in the dramas of the physical plane. Because of this ability, she can help you let go of the ego mind of who you *think* you are based on your patterns and conditioning and help you step into who you *truly* are. She helps you embody your highest expression in this physical form.

If you think about the cervix on a physiological level, it is the bridge between the external world, the conscious (yoni canal) and the internal world, the unconscious (the womb). For this reason, it is linked to the Mystic archetype, who knows how to dance between the physical world of energy and matter and the world of pure consciousness and spirit. When the cervix is activated through orgasmic bliss, the mystic within wakes up. Cervical orgasms are often associated with psychedelic or transcendental orgasms, you may see visions, shapes, colors and have a full-blown mystical experience. These orgasms connect you to higher levels of consciousness through ecstatic bliss... and remind you of who you truly are, as you dissolve into the absolute void space of nothingness and no-mind. The cervix is often very sensitive for two reasons: it doesn't get massaged because of its depth, and/or maybe you have been entered too fast or hard and it has actually been bruised. To de-armor and activate pleasure here we can use either our fingertips or ideally a yoni wand.

What blocks the mystic archetype and thus creates tension or pain in the cervix itself is being shamed or wronged for our intuition, our supernatural abilities, and our sensitivities. This normally happens to us as young children by adults who are frightened by how clearly we can see through to the truth and express and reflect that back to them. I experienced this a lot as a child. I would know things, see things and freely express them to my parents and other adults. I would tell my mother, for instance, when I felt that someone was not trustworthy and she would ignore me, only to find out that this was indeed the truth. I was also heavily shamed for being "too sensitive" as a child. I was told I wouldn't survive in this world if I stayed so sensitive. Sensitivity is the foundation of the mystic, for she is living deeply through her senses and sixth sense, which defies logic. She can pick up on things before they happen, or just have a certain *knowing* about anything. When someone is very sensitive, they also feel a lot more, and feelings are the gateway to information beyond the logical mind. Feelings are conducted by water, and water is the conduit for information from other dimensions and planes of existence. The more someone feels, the more intuitive they will always be. This is why feeling is such a gateway to your intuition, always. As women, we are more deeply feeling and we naturally possess the gifts of intuition and inner knowing. Unfortunately, they often get shut down early in life and we become disconnected from these natural capacities.

Because I began feeling ashamed of my natural abilities as a young girl, I started to shut them down, and like many sensitives and empaths, I began to harden up. The pain of going against my true nature led me to turn to drugs and alcohol to "feel" something again. When I found the spiritual community, I felt like I had finally found somewhere that I was accepted and understood in how deeply I felt, my strong intuition, and my psychic abilities. But as we all know, when you suppress an aspect of yourself for too long, you go to the other side of the spectrum and become the opposite. Because I had suppressed my mystic side for so long, I went to the opposite extreme, living in spiritual communities and becoming so hyper-sensitive that it was actually difficult to function. I was overwhelmed by astral beings on a day-to-day basis. Sometimes I couldn't even leave my home because it felt too difficult having to navigate through so many dimensions. After I ran the course of the mystic on steroids, I slowly began to balance out and have come to a healthy expression of having a foot in both worlds, unseen and the seen; and not suffering from overwhelm or getting too identified with either. I don't believe I need to live in spiritual hubs or spiritual communities to feel "spiritual" anymore—I see the sacred in everything and everywhere. This journey took exploring both sides of the spectrum in order to find equilibrium, and learning how to stay rooted as well as expanded. This is truly the core of the sex priestess: she is rooted in her sex and her priestess, her mystic side and her humanity, her darkness and her light. She does not identify with either; she is fully integrated and embodied in all duality.

Working with the cervix is a big part of balancing the energy of the mystic and activating this archetype into her full expression and power. The cervix is the deepest part of our yoni canal, and it varies in depth from woman to woman. To be clear, I am not saying that if you have a deep cervix you are a deeper woman by any means. We were all born with the most beautiful anatomy that reflects our inner psyche, and if a woman's cervix is much deeper inside of her, it may resemble her inner mystic is much more hidden literally and metaphorically. This could be a psychological and thus physical manifestation of fearing the oracle/mystic/witch archetype, where a woman was persecuted for having these intuitive and psychic gifts. Perhaps a woman's cervix is lower to the yoni entrance because she feels more expressed and safe in this expression of her feminine and she no longer needs to hide herself. Some women can reach it with their full finger inside, but for others, the cervix is further in. I always guide women through a cervix de-armoring self-pleasure practice with the assistance of a beautiful yoni wand. As I mentioned, the cervix is very sensitive and so we want to apply the pressure of the yoni wand very gently over the cervix itself, and allow the emotions to flow, the sensations to be present, and the energy to unlock as any psychological blockages around our mystic archetype are released during this practice. You can find the full cervix/mystic self-pleasure practice inside my online course, Pleasure Principles (see resource link in appendix).

As always, start by exploring intuitively and lovingly on your own. To begin the journey of embodying your mystic archetype and cervical embodiment, work with these journal prompts:

- If you could paint the picture of your inner mystic, who is she? Describe her...
- What does the mystic aspect of you desire the most?
- How does the mystic express herself in your life?
- How can you cultivate more expressions of the mystic in your life?
- What is your relationship to cervical orgasms?
- What are some of the major blocks you experience in the cervical orgasm?
- What parts of yourself are you wishing to die to, those parts you know are not serving you any longer?
- What is holding you back from letting go of these parts of your life?
- Ask your inner mystic: what does true feminine power feel and look like?
- Ask your inner mystic: how connected you feel to your feminine power?
- Ask your inner mystic: what wisdom does she wish to share with you?

Let me assure you, learning to self-pleasure and self-source eros is a journey. Feminine sexuality is a never-ending portal of infinite mystery and pleasure. So wherever you are on your journey, whether it is just starting your own self-pleasure practice, or unlocking internal orgasms; please know that there is no right or wrong way. No orgasm is superior or inferior to another. It does not make you more womanly if you know how to squirt or have cervical orgasms. The key here is to surrender and accept exactly where you are on your own journey. It is through this acceptance and giant exhale you open up to infinite possibilities that await you. It is in the trying and forcing that creates even more shame and contraction, which is what is blocking you from being truly present and accepting of where you uniquely are on your journey.

CODE 5:

ORGASMIC CO-CREATION

Learning to circulate your own sexual energy is an amazing way to bring more pleasure into your life, but it's not just about having more pleasure and vitality. We can also learn to harness this energy into a process of co-creation with life itself to transform our desires into reality.

In Code 5, we are going to explore the unlimited possibilities available to us once we are aware of how to harness this potent force within. It's one thing to learn how to activate our sexual energy as a sex priestess, but the next evolution is learning how to channel this energy into our creativity and everything we came here to birth on the material plane. This is how we move into being the co-creator of our own reality. I say "co-creator" versus creator because I believe there is a humbling process that must take place. We have to recognize that we don't create and achieve things through our will and efforts alone. We are in fact co-creating with a force greater than our minds and egos could ever perceive.

When your sexual and orgasmic energy is flowing through you with zero resistance, you begin stepping into the role of being a co-creator with the divine. How does this work? Your sexuality and orgasmic energy connects you with a frequency of ecstasy, which connects you back to your divine source. You're literally resonating with source and creating from that place. From this frequency, all that is birthed through you, cannot *not* be abundant. Most people reduce the orgasmic frequency just to genital friction or the sexual act, and yes, that is one way to access this frequency. But it's so important to realize that the orgasmic frequency is available to us at all times. Whenever there is flow instead of resistance in your energetic and emotional body, more capacity within is available for the orgasmic frequency to flow. This is what we refer to as being in alignment. Everything is moving smoothly and naturally, and while we are directly in the flow, we do not have to force it. It is from our deepest alignment we are magnetic, clear, radiant and intentional. Becoming devoted to alignment is where all abundance arises from, as we step into the role of co-creating with life itself. This is why we move away from saying we are the "creator" of our reality to rather the *co-creator*, as we are aligning with what is the natural flow of energy that wants to move through us, express through us, and create through us as the vessels of creation.

Flow vs. Resistance: Getting into Alignment

The sex priestess vibrates from her orgasmic frequency, for she knows how to circulate and refine her most vital force of energy within her, self-sourcing from the vertical plane. The number-one way to cultivate more of this orgasmic frequency in your life is to cultivate more pleasure within your body. Pleasure heals, releases tension and trapped energy, and creates strong currents of unobstructed energy flow. It is a high frequency that keeps us in positive states of thought and emotion. We want to strengthen the nervous system through healing our traumas and learning to feel safe in the body because this allows us to hold more—including more pleasure—without becoming overwhelmed. This is a key element of staying in alignment and flow.

Cultivating more pleasure is about doing things that authentically bring you joy. When you are engaged in these activities, you get into a flow state in which you become totally absorbed in the activity and lose track of time. Great artists, writers and musicians often describe the flow states in which they are creating their greatest works as states of union and bliss. It doesn't feel like effort or hard work; there's no sense of drag and drain. There's literally a feeling of flow, as if you are being carried by a current of energy that's bigger than you, and you are completely in the moment. When you are in this timeless space, there is zero resistance in your energetic field and you are in full alignment and co-creation with the universal energy. Much of the time, this completely changes the outcome of the work. More abundance, opportunities and success follows.

In my own life, the distinctions are very clear between when I have created from my mind/ego and when I've created from my body/desire/soul. Writing this book, for example, has been a joyful co-creation with a force beyond myself. Every time I sat behind the keyboard to write, I committed to open my channel up and let the words be written through me as the vessel. I wrote the entire book in about two months, which is quite speedy, and it felt like zero effort at all. I enjoyed the process and never found it draining or difficult. Many times in the past, I found that when new creative ideas knocked on my door (literally, when an idea or concept dropped into my consciousness), if I would then take inspired action to create something, it would always become a success. This includes new workshops, programs, retreats and offerings. This is when I knew I was in alignment and co-creation mode.

The orgasmic frequency gets blocked when we are living out of alignment with what naturally wants to move through us. This happens when we are living from the headspace and doing things out of obligation, fear or guilt. This is the energy of resistance. In this frequency, we are not allowing *shakti* to flow through us. Our vibration lowers and we are less able to co-create with the universal flow of energy. Instead, we are creating from our mind and ego, and we have to work twice as hard to try to do it all ourselves and attempt to control the outcome instead of letting life support us. When we do this, we fall into the hustle paradigm. This happens when we're over-efforting and over-exerting ourselves from a place of control, focusing on the quantity of output, and it's all a numbers game. This is when we are addicted to the never-ending rat race and never feel satisfied, as we are creating from the horizontal plane and out of touch with our true soul's essence. No matter what we create from this place, it is never enough because it doesn't truly nourish us, and because the process of creation is one that depletes rather than energizes us. Everything feels forced, clunky, and like teeth-pulling hard work.

I have created most things in my life from a place of flow and alignment—but not everything. Sometimes I would create something from my mind/ego and it was often out of a lack or fear mentality, or a sense of obligation or "should." I would later realize that this was the case when the offering would inevitably fail. I would have zero sign-ups and it just felt like work or forcing. This has always been my guiding truth: if it flows and is effortless, it is in alignment with my soul. If it feels hard or forceful, it is something created from ego and lack. The universe is always responding to the energy we put out. You will quickly learn that you really cannot fool the universe once you start playing in these realms of creation.

Take out your journal and do some self-reflection around when in your life you're in a state of flow and alignment, and when you're in a state of resistance.

- Write out a list of the activities, people and places that bring you the most pleasure. What activities get you into those flow states where you lose track of time?
- Write out a list of activities, people, places and projects you are engaging in that do not bring you genuine fulfillment and joy. What are you doing out of obligation, fear, guilt or a sense of "should"?
- Ask yourself: Are you willing to let go of these people, places, activities and projects? What actions would need to be taken in order to do so? What's one thing that you can lovingly release from your life to make space for greater flow?

Returning to Our Feminine Nature

Most people have been conditioned into creating and living from the limited plane of the mental sphere. We are born into societies, governments and education systems that always enforce *logos*, the masculine principle, over *eros*, the feminine principle. We are brainwashed into believing that logic and the masculine principle is the key to succeeding and winning in life. The entire society is built up favoring the masculine principle alone, completely devoid of the feminine aspect of creation, which ironically is the true force behind creating anything in this world! But because our entire society is based upon masculine principles, we know no other way—*until we do*.

I grew up going to an all-girls catholic high school, where the motto was, ironically, "Women can do anything." It was implied that this was anything, except being truly feminine. Even in this all-female environment, logic and intellect was extremely valued and prized, and considered far superior and respected over anything linked to creativity and expression. Subjects like economics, physics and mathematics were worth their weight in gold, far surpassing what were deemed inferior subjects like art, music, home economics, and dance. Anything creative and right-brained was considered "just entertainment"—not anything you could create a real career out of in the modern world. Women who chose to drop out of high school and study things like hairdressing, fashion, or the arts were viewed as "drop outs." The school's messaging was that this path would "get you nowhere in life." Clearly, the conditioning ran deep. For those like myself who chose to finish school and enter the "real world" of university and careers in the fields of medicine, economics, finance, business, we were doing what we believed and were taught would bring us success, and the basic respect of being a worthy human being on this planet.

Nadine Lee

The great awakening and the crumbling of the delusions instilled by institutions happens for many around this time of starting their adult lives and their careers. This was certainly the case for me. I was waking up to the fact that this societal brainwashing is a trap that leads us to waste our true human potential and creative expression (while creating debt, might I add). I did the thing, went to university, completed my bachelor of business and worked for a couple of years in advertising and marketing. It wasn't long before I realized that this linear way of living, creating and doing life was completely suppressing my spirit and true creative potential. I couldn't stand doing the same thing every single day, working the same hours, going to the same location. I started to feel dead inside. I remember looking at my bosses who had been doing this lifestyle for over a decade and realizing I had zero aspiration to end up like them—stressed, depleted, haggard and lacking in life force.

I knew I desired to live a life that supported my feminine nature, which was cyclical, and allowed me to create from a deeper part of myself which was not logical or quantified. I knew that I required spaciousness to birth. Just like a woman takes nine months to birth the greatest creation of all—a child—so too do we as women need spaciousness to birth all our other projects, such as books, courses, businesses and creative projects. Living life in this feminine flow is not linear, and it is definitely not predictable or "safe." But once the feminine calls you into the body out of the mind, to refuse the call is to betray yourself. You are given the opportunity to become the co-creator of your life in partnership with this divine force that is forever longing to penetrate you with all the abundance and creative inspiration you could ever imagine.

The transition from my corporate life into entrepreneurship was a big one that required me to deconstruct so many beliefs I had about myself. I was groomed since I was a child to live life in a certain expected and predictable way: day in and day out, Monday to Friday, you show up to an institution, from school to university to the office. You put in your hours and receive your reward. To leave that life behind, I had to undo 20+ years of brainwashing and programming. But when you get the call to find another way, even if you don't even know how or what it is yet, you must listen. All I knew was that I didn't want the 9-to-5 corporate life. I desired a life that was creative, one that worked with my feminine cyclical nature. By committing to this, I surrendered and let life figure out *how* it happened. This was not an easy feat. As I said, I had to break down so many conditionings I held. I remember saying that I am not a risk taker, and even if I find a career path I am passionate about, I would prefer to work for someone else. That was a major belief I had to deconstruct. Here I am almost 15 years later, working solely for myself as CEO of my own company. I believe that where there is a will, there is always a way. The will is the divine will speaking through your desires, inviting you to step outside of all you know and believe and follow that fire that has been ignited within. This is when we step into our true dharma, when we let go of who we *think* we are and become who we truly are.

In her fullest expression, the feminine is an open receptive channel. Her longing and desire for more in life at the deepest level is the longing to be penetrated by pure consciousness itself. When she becomes fully open and allows herself to be filled with pure consciousness, she begins to embody the role of the co-creator, working with the divine masculine as she births through her clear, open and receptive womb. David Deida, an international author and teacher on masculine and feminine dynamics, speaks about how the feminine seeks to be filled, whereas the masculine seeks emptiness. However, there are two clear distinctions with this, the immature feminine wants more on the horizontal physical plane—nothing ever satiates her thirst and she will extract more out of men and the universe at large in her confusions, yet never feel deeply fulfilled. Instead, she feels entitled. The mature feminine wants more from the divine masculine. She is more concerned with humbling and gracefully receiving from the vertical plane, self-sourcing from source/God/the divine itself, and she also embraces sacred union with men to reconnect to God through their merging. Being able to hold and receive more requires her to feel fully inhabited and safe enough in her body to truly let go and open to receive through the feminine womb channel. This is why the energetic state of the womb and yoni are a clear indication if we are truly inhabiting the body and feeling safe or not. Lovemaking tells us exactly what is going on. If a woman's yoni is even slightly tense when penetrated by the masculine, or if her body contracts, even on the slightest level, she holds those contractions and blocks herself from receiving from all of creation. She can't fully let go beyond that threshold because she doesn't feel safe in her body and subconsciously she has chosen a man she knows she cannot let go fully with. If, however, she has a strong connection with God and the divine masculine, her choice in men will reflect this frequency of the divine masculine and her body will respond accordingly. A woman's choice of men, and also her ability to co-create, is a reflection of her inner union, whereby she needs a strong inner masculine in order to feel safe and strong enough to be surrendered to life itself. Co-creation doesn't only come from feminine receptivity. It's not just about being passive and waiting around for the universe to drop the right opportunity in her lap; rather, co-creation is a balance of masculine action and feminine receptivity. We need a strong personal will, which is developed through a healthy inner masculine force, to effectively surrender to divine will and follow divine guidance, which reflects our relationship to our inner feminine essence. The two co-create harmoniously with a power beyond.

When it comes to lovemaking, she is fully surrendered and can drop into a place of total trust. At the point of crossing the threshold beyond what she knows, she can fully let go because her nervous system truly feels rested, safe and at ease; she is truly inhabiting her body. This is why we begin with the work of clearing the womb portal of suppressed emotions that are blocking this miraculous portal of creation, as this is critical to feeling safe in our bodies and open to receive. This is also why the work with self-pleasure and yoni de-armoring is essential to becoming this orgasmic co-creator and deepest embodiment of the feminine. These codes live inside our bodies, specifically inside our feminine portal of power: our womb and yoni. Our birthright is to tap into this feminine power to materialize our heart's desires.

Creator Codes & Wealth Codes

When the feminine is fully inhabiting her portal of power, her yoni and womb, she offers herself up as a bridge of creation. Every month as she ovulates, she asks the universe: *What wants to be birthed through me this month?* When she listens to this guidance, it is impossible for abundance not to flow through her. This is because when she is creating from this place of power and alignment, from her very womb itself, the creation is aligned with the energy of all of creation and nature, which is total abundance. Nature is extremely abundant! One tiny seed creates an entire tree with thousands of fruits over many years. Co-creating with source leads to abundance in all its expressions, including money, but most importantly the deepest level of fulfillment and inner richness.

When women tell me that they want to activate their wealth codes, I always say that it comes hand-in-hand with activating your creator codes, which is ultimately the embodiment of your deepest feminine energy. The feminine is the creator. She is the one with the womb who births new life into this world.

Money is simply one expression of the abundance of creation, and yet it's a very important one that women are only now truly beginning to be the custodians of.

Money is simply a medium of giving and receiving; it's a current of energy that flows back to you when you are offering your gifts to this world. This is why your money flow is directly linked to your relationship to the feminine. When you come into right relation with your feminine essence by truly inhabiting your sexuality, your body and your emotions, money flows in and out in balance. Why? Because when women reclaim their sexual sovereignty, they simultaneously reclaim their birthright to wealth. Sexually sovereign and empowered women know how to circulate their sexual energy. When sexual energy is circulating, when the force of creation is flowing, so is money. When sexual energy is circulating, shame, victim consciousness and scarcity—the biggest blocks to money—do not exist. When sexual energy is circulating, she has unplugged from the false matrix of society which creates wealth from the mental realm, which is inherently limiting. (Even if we manage to generate a lot of money from a mental space it will not bring the true sense of abundance that we are searching for.) Instead, she is rooted into the true matrix of the earth, plugged into the deepest support and infinite abundance of Gaia, as she creates from the quantum realm of womb consciousness. Her true creatrix codes come fully online. When her sexual energy is flowing, she is connected to Source on the vertical axis, self-sourcing life force from the divine versus, as we've discussed, the horizontal way of sourcing energy that most humans are stuck in (sourcing from overeating, artificial stimulants, seeking validation and empty sex with other depleted humans). When she is self-sourcing, anything she creates from her creatrix womb center, will naturally lead to abundance, because she is creating from her open surrendered vessel, offering her womb as the bridge between worlds, birthing creations that are of true service to the world.

The balance of wealth is finally tipping back into the hands of women after ages of suppression of female sexuality and thus her creatrix and wealth potential. As women remember and reawaken their sacred sexual sovereignty, I have seen many times that unlimited wealth flows their way. We are living in exciting times full of new possibilities. I love witnessing my clients and more women in this world awakening to their sacred sexuality and unlocking their creativity and wealth codes to become the powerful creators they truly are. Money is an energetic tool with the power to create great change, and it's moving more and more into the hands of conscious, heart-centered beings—where it belongs.

When I worked in the corporate world for those first few years of my adult life, I would live paycheck to paycheck, under the delusional "safety" of my 9-5, Monday-to-Friday corporate job. Yes, this felt "secure" in a certain way, but it's a trap designed by the false matrix of the mind. You know that every two weeks you get X amount of dollars deposited into your bank account, but you have no room to expand beyond that dollar amount. Your wealth potential is capped at that number. This is unbelievably limiting. When I look back on this way of operating and creating in the world, from that logical masculine way of being, I can see how much it held me back. The feminine desires to expand as much as possible, which has no cap!

When I took the plunge into entrepreneurship 11 years ago (something I said I would "never do" because I believed I wasn't a risk taker), I shifted from the illusion of safety from logos, the mental sphere and the predictable matrix, to a new world of many unknowns. I faced real questions: Where is my paycheck going to come from? How much will flow in each month? Will I be able to maintain the lifestyle I want for myself? It took a lot of reprogramming of my beliefs around money, and most importantly, my trust in the universe and my role as a co-creator and the feminine mystery. Now I am making far beyond what I could have ever made in those corporate jobs—while actually enjoying the world I do and sharing something genuinely meaningful. The sky's the limit full of creative potential as I align with continuously trusting, surrendering and co-creating with the divine force. Trust and surrender are feminine frequencies, so anyone who is living in this realm (artists, entrepreneurs, visionaries) are embodying the feminine frequency. Most people desire to live their wildest dreams, to become a co-creator with the divine, but to actually do it takes a lot of courage. It's not easy to trust and take a big risk. I truly believe that this is every single person's birthright, but we've been deluded away from it through this heavily programmed video game we call life. To be a co-creator takes trusting in nature, and in your own true nature. The feminine frequency goes beyond logos and the mental sphere and the false matrix of society and plugs you into the true womb matrix of the earth and cosmos, that only desires to nourish all of you. Where do you think all abundance and resources that support us comes from? The Earth—nowhere else. And yes, this includes money. When I guide women into feminine embodiment and energetics, their life takes a 180, because anything not aligned with truth dissolves. From this place you become a co-creator of this entire game of life, surrendered and living in accordance with a force completely beyond your logical mind.

Co-Creating Your Soul's Desires

In order to be in co-creation with the divine, we must empty ourselves out and become that clear channel for the orgasmic energy of life to flow through us. The orgasmic energy is always flowing through all of creation. It is the energy that is indeed responsible for all of life—when the bee lands upon a flower, or the waves come crashing upon the sandy shore, or a volcano erupts and clears the fertile ground beneath it. This energy flows freely throughout nature, and we can see that nature is always operating in perfect harmony and always seeking and achieving homeostasis, even if the ecosystem has been tipped off-balance by human intervention. Nature is always attempting to restore the balance of all energies and return to natural abundance and flow. This energy also flows through humans, as we are not separate from nature. As it flows freely through our body vessels, we tap into the universal flow and become that co-creator with existence itself. This is when we feel "in the flow" or "in alignment."

What blocks this natural flow of orgasmic energy moving through us humans is density in our energy, emotional and physical bodies. The physical body gets blocked by toxins from processed food and chemicals; the emotional body gets blocked by toxicity of unprocessed traumas and suppressed emotions; and then the mental body gets blocked by toxins created from negative thought patterns and carrying other people's energies in our field. If you can imagine, there is a central channel, like a tube, that runs down the spine. This is where the orgasmic creative energy wants to flow. When there are no stuck emotions and physical toxins, this tube is fully unblocked and the creative orgasmic waters can flow freely through the whole system, nourishing the body and chakras and then being channeled into our creative expressions. When these toxins and emotional debris build up, however, the orgasmic creative energy gets stuck. It is obstructed and cannot flow through. This is when people experience stagnation, a lack of energy or drive, lack of libido, feeling lackluster and just generally dead inside. The life force is blocked, so in a sense, they are dead, or at least not fully alive. Tantra is all about purifying the physical, emotional and energy bodies so this orgasmic creative energy can flow freely through you.

Once we are operating from a clear channel, it is very easy then to tap into our core soul desires. When I talk about orgasmic co-creation, I'm not talking about manifesting a new car or a fancy vacation (although there is nothing inherently wrong with those things). It is about creating what will truly nourish you and will nourish the world through you. There is a distinct difference between the desires of the ego and soul desires. The egoic desires are usually focused on self-serving pursuits. The ego is not all bad and should be banished, but instead, it's a matter of harnessing this powerful force. In yogic philosophy, there are three types of ego: 1) Tamasic ego, which is self-destructive and blind; 2) Rajasic ego, which is self-centered and self-serving; and 3) Sattvic ego, which is creative and protective. Thus, our aim should not be to get rid of the ego entirely, but to move towards the Sattvic ego over the other types, and to use it to our advantage when it serves us for good. To keep ourselves in integrity when it comes to egoic desires, we can determine which category the desire falls into: Tamasic, Rajasic or Sattvic.

The soul, on the other hand, is the part of ourselves that exists when the ego self has taken a step back. A state in which the soul has taken over is often described as a flow state where external constructs like time no longer exist. The soul might be regarded as your "true nature," since this is the essence of who you are beyond labels, expectations or judgments. It just *is*. When your desires come from your soul, it is as if a force beyond logic and reason takes over and longs to move through you. It may not make any sense at all to your rational mind, but you will have a sense that you have to follow it. These desires can be recognized by the deep sense that they are somehow bigger or beyond us, and the feeling that we *must* follow them. I believe that the ego and soul can work harmoniously together. In fact, this is the ultimate union of opposites, much like masculine and feminine. There is only an issue when one side takes dominance over the other. When it comes to our desires, we can receive guidance from our soul's desires and allow our sattvic ego to act as the servant to the soul. Then the ego becomes the driving force to accomplish divine guidance, which is exactly what it should be. The issue is only when the ego is just running the show at the expense of the soul, pursuing selfish desires that ultimately don't bring fulfillment or joy.

When we are clear on our desires, it is very easy to then co-create, as these core soul desires are the very seeds of co-creation. Our desires are not a bad thing that will lead us astray. I believe that our desires, especially when established from a conscious clear channel, are the gateways to our evolution. Whatever we desire is valid and is leading us to our ultimate liberation. Even a monk who says he has no desires still desires to reach enlightenment. We all have different desires, according to whatever soul contracts we came here to fulfill and where we are on our unique soul path. I have never been one to shun desires, or shame them, and in fact, the path of tantra encourages desires to be expressed and harnessed. Tantra is also about the transformation of the raw energy of desire, and learning to use this energy to accelerate the process of spiritual development. Desires are meant to be expressed, and expressing our desires can free up a lot of dense energy in the emotional and energetic bodies. If we are holding onto or repressing any form of desire, this blocks our channel even more.

It's important to be clear about what we desire, and to get curious about it. But we must be aware that what we desire often is not the thing we are seeking or desiring, but actually *how we think we will feel once we attain that desire*. For example, if we desire to be in partnership, we are actually seeking the frequency beneath the physical manifestation of partnership—so we are seeking to experience the frequencies of union, love, contentment and bliss. (These frequencies are in fact the orgasmic frequencies, the highest level emotions associated with any desire.)

When we are looking to orgasmically co-create with the universe, there are a few stages:

1. Purification of the emotional and physical bodies
2. Getting clear on desires
3. Surrendering to the orgasmic frequency
4. Sexual alchemy

Purification

Purification of the physical body starts with cleaning up your diet, reducing toxin exposure and clearing out old emotional baggage. In addition to the basic everyday tips below, I would also add powerful detoxification protocols such as parasite and liver cleanses twice a year. These are essential for the modern day we are living in.

Here are some of the most important things you can do to kickstart your journey of physical purification:

1. Cutting out all refined sugar: Sugar is truly the devil, in my opinion. I am referring here to white refined sugar that has been stripped back of any nutrients. Refined sugar spikes your blood sugar to rapid highs, and then plummets to rapid lows, which leaves you feeling hooked and addicted. Sugar is extremely addictive, and it's been said that it may even be more addictive than some hard drugs like cocaine and MDMA. It dehydrates you, ages you and elevates blood pressure, not to mention affecting your mood. Studies on mental health patients have shown that when their sugar intake was reduced, their symptoms also radically diminished. It's not about deprivation. Everything in moderation—a little bit of sugar here and there won't harm you. But try adopting natural sweeteners such as raw honey, dates, and monk fruit. Your body will thank you.

2. Ditching pharmaceuticals: The majority of people in developed countries around the world use pharmaceutical drugs. The global pharmaceutical market has experienced significant growth in recent years, with the total global pharmaceutical market valued at about 1.42 trillion U.S. dollars in 2021. This is a significant increase from 2001, when the market was valued at just 390 billion U.S. dollars. This industry is a business, and as you can see, it's a very lucrative business that feeds off your sickness. Pharmaceutical drugs are band-aid solutions that mask your symptoms temporarily, keeping you sick and never actually addressing the root of the disease itself. This industry *wants* you to stay sick, because if you get well, they would go out of business. Whenever you experience any sort of physical dis-ease, consider whether it's truly necessary to rush straight to the doctor's office and get a prescription. Sometimes pharmaceutical drugs are necessary and unavoidable, but most of the time they are not. Be informed about your options and consider alternative therapies, such as homeopathy, naturopathy and nutrition, which address the root cause of illness. There are times when Western medicine is beneficial and needed, but much more often, there are other, healthier ways that we can address physical imbalances. Combined with addressing emotional dis-ease through modalities we have addressed in this book and even working with a somatic therapist, as emotions are almost always at the root of physical disease. When your body learns how to self-heal, you begin to trust it more deeply, and your channel becomes more clear of any artificial interference.

3. Reducing red meat intake: There is nothing wrong with eating meat, but again—everything in moderation. Too much red meat can create acidity and inflammation in the body. If you choose to consume red meat, it is best to source the highest quality possible, grass-fed and organic. If a cow was brutally slaughtered, the frequency of that painful death is carried in the flesh of the animal, so that is what you are consuming.

This affects us on very subtle levels as humans who consume. In tribal days, we would go out and hunt our own meat, and it was a much more humane process, with a couple of tools versus a slaughterhouse. If you want to eat meat (not just red meat but any kind of meat), make it a priority to source from small, local organic farms, which tend to use more humane methods, instead of factory-farmed industrial agriculture. This will also support you if you choose to consume meat.

4. Drinking clean filtered water: Our bodies are made up of 80% water. Without water, we would die. We can survive for weeks without food, but without water, we would perish quickly. It's important to be conscious about the quality of your drinking water, because not all water is created equal. The tap water available in our homes can be contaminated with all sorts of poisons such as fluoride, lead, chlorine and other chemicals that block your pineal gland, and thus affect your capacity to think clearly and tap into your intuition. It is best to source spring water if possible (direct from the spring is the ultimate, if you can find access!). However, if you do not have access to a spring closeby, getting a high-quality water filtration system installed in your house that eliminates fluoride and contaminants is essential for good health and a clear physical body channel. Ditching plastic water bottles and replacing them with copper or flasks is also essential for good health, as the chemicals from plastics actually seep into your water and contaminate it even more.

5. Sourcing organic fruits and vegetables: The fruits and vegetables that we see on most grocery store shelves have been so genetically modified (as a way to preserve shelf life) that the amount of actual nutrients you are receiving is miniscule. They have also been sprayed with chemicals and pesticides that harm our health. When you eat this kind of produce, you are mainly consuming hormones that have been pumped into the piece of fruit or vegetable to preserve it and make it look like a beautifully manicured item on a shelf. When most people look at organic fruits and vegetables, they are shocked. The size is much smaller, and there are discolorations, wormholes, bumps and nicks that show that it is a real piece of fruit or vegetable grown naturally and organically without interference. This produce holds way more actual nutritional value. Try visiting your local farmer's markets on the weekend, where farmers come in and sell their produce direct from farm to you, cutting out the middleman—big supermarkets. The quality you will find is worth every single penny. What you put in your body matters!

6. Eliminating all processed foods: When I look at fast food, I do not even consider this real food. It is merely a sugar infested, genetically modified, chemically pumped flavor explosion that sends your brain into overdrive and your blood sugar spiking and sadly leaves you addicted for more. This also goes for packaged foods. If you cannot understand or pronounce most of the items on the ingredients list, do not put it in your body.

7. Detoxifying the Emotional Body: Purification of the emotional body is a process of developing a healthy relationship with your emotions and inner world. Set up daily check-ins with yourself and create space to feel what wants to be felt, simply witnessing the emotion as energy in motion. It is not about going into the story of each emotion, but just witnessing without judgment as any emotion begins to arise. Once the emotion can be felt fully through, expressed through the body through breath sounds and movement, it has the chance to liberate and be alchemised completely from the emotional body itself. For us as women, our menstrual cycle is such a potent time for this emotional body purification and alchemy process, mentioned in code 1. You'll be amazed at how clearing out old emotions makes you feel more clear, vibrant and energized.

With your physical and emotional bodies becoming more clear, it is much easier to listen to the whispers of your heart and soul. With clarity of mind, free from pollutants and pineal gland blockers, the clarity of your desires speak in very subtle but powerful ways.

Clarity of Desires

Once the channel is clear, the next phase of orgasmic co-creation is to get clear on your core soul desires. These core soul desires live in the deepest part of your soul, yoni and womb. In this next process, it is not about *thinking* your desires into fruition, but rather *feeling* what truly inspires you—what it is you are deeply longing for from the depths of your feminine soul and clear, aligned channel. If you're not sure what your soul's desires are, you can find clues in what is naturally unfolding for you and also in what excites you the most. The number one way I can hear my soul's desires speaking to me is by listening to what brings me the highest level of excitement. When I tap into the possibility of that desire manifesting, I will feel a lightness in my entire physical and energy bodies, and an excitable feeling. Often my yoni will speak to me and it will feel like a turned-on sensation. This is what I listen to more than my head. The egoic desires speak from the mind, whereas the soul desires speak through the body. As women specifically, they speak through our yoni. This is why we did so much work around clearing the trauma in the yoni and clearing the emotional debris in the womb—so this channel is clear, and her voice can be heard loud and clear. Once you have unlocked this, your yoni is literally the only oracle you will ever need in life.

For this next self-reflection journaling, I am going to ask you what your deepest desires are for the major areas of your life. Take a moment to drop into your body, deep into your womb and yoni, and feel what turns you on the most as you make your way through each core area of your life. Feel into what excites you the most and feels super expansive in your physical, emotional and energetic bodies. Feel free to take out your journal now, create some sacred space and get clear on what it is you are longing for in these core areas:

- Relationship desire
- Career desire
- Health desire
- Money desire
- Creativity desire

Surrendering to the Orgasmic Frequency

Once your desires have been made clear, it is now about tapping into that orgasmic frequency, which is essentially the highest-level emotion associated with each desire. When you can focus on and cultivate these high-frequency emotions, you'll start to become a vibrational match for the physical manifestation to take place. This helps tremendously in co-creating it into existence with the divine. This orgasmic frequency is essentially the free-flowing life force energy that is expansive and moving through all of life. It wants to move through you, it wants to move through everything to nourish it and create through it. When you feel the most expansive emotion, the highest possible level of excitement associated with each desire, then you will feel a taste of that orgasmic frequency moving through you. It is an incredibly expansive feeling and definitely not confined to genital friction or the act of sex. As I mentioned, it is always moving through all of life, pervading everything and everyone. This is the energy that fuels the co-creation process, transforming desire into reality.

Now, for each desire in each area of your life, feel the way you would long to feel if these things were to manifest. For example, if your current soul desire for your career is to be a famous Ted-X speaker, how would that make you feel at the highest frequency of emotion? Write that next to each one of the desires you have listed:

- Relationship desire + Orgasmic frequency (how would this make you feel?)
- Career desire + Orgasmic frequency (how would this make you feel?)
- Health desire + Orgasmic frequency (how would this make you feel?)
- Money desire + Orgasmic frequency (how would this make you feel?)
- Creativity desire + Orgasmic frequency (how would this make you feel?)

Sexual Alchemy

The final phase of orgasmic co-creation is sexual alchemy. This is about activating our sexual energy and starting to move it through the body—which is now a clear open channel—and align it with these core soul desires and orgasmic frequency.

Start by creating a ritual space to go through the above process of getting clear on your desires, connecting with the orgasmic frequency of the emotions, and then surrendering and releasing them. That means stating what you want to the universe, or the divine, and then letting it go completely. Then you'll start to move into activating your erotic energy through self-pleasuring. But you're not going into self-pleasure with any goal to get your manifestation to come to fruition—no. You are simply allowing your eros to continue to purify your channel and amplify your energetic and magnetic field to those desires you have already stated to the universe and surrendered to.

It is very important we don't move into "using" our sexual energy to gain something, as this takes out the entire joy of allowing erotic energy to move through your body for the sake of pleasure and love. Doing the preparation reflection work of getting clear on your desires and their orgasmic frequency emotions is enough. Then you can go into self-pleasure, purely for pleasure knowing that it is naturally amplifying your desires. Again, this is about being in the feminine frequency—rather than trying to control the outcome, we learn to let go, trust, and let ourselves be supported by a force greater than ourselves.

Co-creation is truly our birthright state of being. We were meant to be a completely clear channel, aligned with the universal flow of energy that is always moving through all of life. When we begin to attune to this frequency, is when we are living in full alignment and in orgasmic co-creation. We are surrendered to a higher force that wants to create through us, trusting our soul's core desires as gateways to our ultimate liberation and love. This leads us to our next code: becoming the initiatrix of awakening. When our channel is open and we are a vessel of creation, we have the capacity to awaken those around us through our healing energy, touch and presence.

CODE 6:
INITIATRIX OF AWAKENING

Sex Priestess

When we heal ourselves and activate our own vital energy and feminine power, we become the force of nature that we naturally are as women—capable not only of co-creating our own reality, but also being a healing and transforming presence for others. A sex priestess begins her journey by coming home to her own body and healing her traumas, strengthening her connection to the divine, and learning to manage her own energy flow. Then, she can help others connect to their divine nature.

Through this journey of unlocking our feminine body codes, we begin to extend our life force to penetrate every inch of our reality. As a woman comes to embody the sex priestess, she naturally becomes an initiatrix of awakening—one who initiates others into their fully awakened and embodied potential. This is especially true for men, of course; but not only men. She becomes a potential healing and activating force to everyone she comes in contact with. This is fundamentally because her embodiment and her eros—the most powerful force there is—is freely flowing through her entire being. When this code is unlocked, the sex priestess is activated not only in lovemaking, but in every interaction with men. Simply being in her presence connects him to the divine feminine and activates his eros, and she knows how to support the alchemy of this energy for awakening.

The sex priestess initiates others into the hidden knowledge of sacred sexuality and the body temple, as she has healed the split between matter and spirit within herself. As you know, this archetype is fully unlocked when we merge our primal essence (sexuality) with our higher essence (spirituality). However, we have been conditioned to separate the two and most people live in this state of separation. This is obvious if you look at the core of most religions. The classic examples are the Eve-Lilith split and the Madonna-Whore complex, which disconnects women from their sexuality (darkness, Lilith, Mary Magdalen), in favor of more purity and obedience (light, Eve, the Virgin Mary). Lilith is the archetype of the repressed, dark, wild feminine. She was the first wife of Adam in the Garden of Eden, and, as the story goes, was cast aside and replaced by Eve because her dominance and assertion displeased Adam. Lilith represents the darker parts of our collective femininity that have been cast aside and labeled as unwomanly and unworthy as women were taught that they should be obedient and pure. The energy of Lilith is intense, activating and fiery, and it is that aspect of the feminine that all men (and humanity in fact) long for yet are so afraid to face. It is her sacred fire and rage that is the energy transmuted into true personal power and the empowerment of others around her. So long as we repress this aspect within our own psyche, through rejecting it in the outside embodiment of the wild dark feminine, we are forever rejecting our true power within.

Similarly, the Madonna-Whore complex reflects the Church's rejection of Mary Magdalen (Jesus's consort and a priestess of sacred sexuality who was labeled a whore by the church) in favor of a Mother Mary who is obedient, pure, virginal and self-sacrificing. The darkness, the body, and sexuality is rejected in favor of the feminine as mother and virgin.

In actuality, both light and dark feminine, Eve and Lilith, the Virgin Mary and Mary Magdalen, sex and spirit can be merged into union and met at the melting pot of all duality—the heart. With this code, we heal the duality within ourselves at the deepest possible level. The core of this code is releasing shame around our erotic feminine essence, and our wild eros, as she expresses through the dark feminine, the sacred prostitute, the Lilith archetype within. This archetype holds the ultimate key to your erotic liberation and integration of the fullest spectrum of your femininity and power. As long as we are living in the fragmented split between Eve and Lilith, playing the good girl, the good subservient wife, ignoring the primal underbelly flames of liberation inside of us, we are not able to truly step into our fullest power and ultimate expression—and we cannot access our true potential to heal and awaken others. For the dark is what gives us substance, the feminine is the darkness, she is the substance, the matter, the Earth—so to deny the dark feminine especially is to deny your true feminine.

I have held countless workshops and retreats on feminine embodiment, and we always do archetypal embodiment work at the core of my offerings. I've found that this archetype is always the one through which women find their true liberation. When they allow themselves to just unleash their wild, erotic, sexy, unfiltered, untamed self—free from judgement or concerns of how they look or are perceived—something deep and potent gets unlocked. Years of suppressing this force in an attempt to "fit in" and live according to others' expectations of her, out of fear of love being withdrawn if she speaks her truth gets unlocked. She finds her power through embodying the darker feminine aspect of herself. For when this aspect is repressed, the dark feminine gets shoved down so far in the psyche AND in the body that it blocks the erotic energy from flowing through a woman and she may end up passive aggressive or depressed because she feels she is betraying herself consistently. She has spent her life pleasing everyone but herself. I truly believe that liberating the dark feminine is the key to women's and society's liberation.

Here is the truth: sex is a gateway to the divine. The two are not mutually exclusive. In order to be one with the divine, we do not need to cut off our connection to our sexuality. What a bizarre concept our institutions have brainwashed us with. And yet it also makes perfect sense: the leaders of organized religions always knew that our sexual energy is the most powerful force we have access to. To cut people off from their power and to get them to give their power away to the hierarchy of the church, they created a story of sexuality being dirty and shameful. The fact that we are conceived from the divine through such a sacred act should be proof enough of its power and divinity. To think that once we are born, we are disconnected from the source from which we came from and the act that gave us life, makes no sense.

Conception is the ultimate union of sex and spirit. When we fragment the two as we enter this earthly dimension, we fragment ourselves from wholeness to separation. The distortions around sex on this planet are absurd. The religions teach us it's a sin, the governments regulate it and turn marriage into a business, and the media and corporations hyper-sexualise and commodify it to sell us their products. No wonder everyone is confused. And the truth is, when there is confusion around one's sexuality—the essence and core power of us—people are much easier to manipulate. This is the oldest trick in the book. When someone is fully sexually sovereign, they are an empowered being who will not be dictated by outside authorities. They are a free thinker, sovereign in the truest sense of the word. Reclaiming one's sexual sovereignty is about restoring one's erotic innocence. It's about remembering that we are not fragmented and reclaiming our inner knowing that our sexual energy isn't dirty or sinful. To me, sexuality feels like a frequency of play and curiosity. Why does it have to turn bitter and twisted as one grows up? Why does such shame have to be laced around our curiosity and innocence? Why do we take on these conditionings and distorted beliefs in our subconscious through religions, governments and media? The process of reclaiming your sexual sovereignty is obviously a journey and it's likely a big part of the reason why you are reading this book. It is about reclaiming all the shadow aspects from the distortions that brainwashed us in the first place, to finally meet back in the heart space, where sex and spirit unite, and erotic innocence is finally restored. Here in the heart resides the sex priestess (the union of opposites). She is a guardian of the ancient wisdom of sacred sexuality which has been completely hidden and buried in our culture. When she activates this code, she will come to fully embody this wisdom and awaken it in others.

This requires that she explore the shadow dynamics from the distortions around her sexuality in order to truly reclaim her sexual sovereignty. That's what the story of Perspephone is about. This is a myth told of a young girl named Kore who was the Goddess of spring, reigning over life, flowers and new growth and renewal. One day she was playing in her garden joyfully, as it was here that she could hold her power as she reigned as Goddess, in the lightness of existence. However, the story teaches us that to truly hold our power, we must be able to hold our power in the darkest of places, not just in the light. So the story goes, Kore gets kidnapped by Hades, the God of the Underworld. He plucks her from her blissful garden in the upper world, into the pits of hell the underworld where he and many demons reside. Here she has to find her power, and reign as a Goddess of not just the upper world, but the underworld also. She becomes Perspephone, Queen of the Underworld, spending six months of the year in darkness, and Goddess of Spring, spending the other six months in the light. This is what brings her into the fullness of her integrated power—fearless, unshakable, unfuckwithable anywhere—in both the light and the dark.

This story has always rung so true through my own explorations of the light and dark aspects of my own psyche. Persephone's story is such a potent teaching about learning to hold mastery over not just our conscious selves (light), but more importantly our unconscious selves (dark). For it is through exploring and liberating our unconscious darkness that we make way for so much more light consciousness to be anchored within us. The experience of having made these underworld descents into the unconscious is the difference between someone who is truly in their power versus someone who is all "love and light" and avoiding the darkness within (aka spiritual bypassing). True power is to be found in someone who is whole, who has explored their dark side, the unconscious terrains within, traversed them, fought their own inner demons and thus truly found their strength by overcoming that which binds them in their unconscious. One of the most common parts of ourselves that gets trapped in the unconscious is our relationship to our sexuality, for reasons that we've been discussing throughout this book and especially all the sexual abuse and shame riddling our collective consciousness. I honestly believe that the journey of healing our sexuality is the key to our ultimate liberation, for it is here we reclaim those exiled parts of us and bring them to the light. We get to face off with our inner demons, like the story of Persephone shows us—not actual demons in hell, but metaphorically the demons inside of us being the repressed and exiled parts of us we believe will never be loved and accepted: the shame, the guilt, the fear, the ugly emotions associated with painful experiences around our sexuality. When we face them head-on, they no longer have power over us. We are finally free.

Meeting the Dark Feminine

The dark feminine was one of my inner demons and one that lives in many women's unconscious, waiting to be met and integrated into her psyche. And when I use the term "dark feminine" I am not referring to darkness in the sense of evil or bad, but more darkness as a representation of what is not yet brought to the light, so it is another term for the unconscious. It is the sacred prostitute, the holy whore, the slut, the seductress, the medusa—these parts that are so repressed in women and society at large, and yet come out in all sorts of unhealthy ways when not consciously explored. As I shared in the last chapter, it was during my time living in my witch's cabin deep in the Byron Bay hinterland that I was first introduced to my dark feminine. The alchemy that was happening within me was palpable and I was living and breathing shakti as I communed so closely with the earth during this time. From my outdoor baths under the stars, to letting my body hair grow wild, to communing with all the wild animals that I shared that land with, including the python and a wild black cat. Pure life force energy was pulsing through me and I was unleashing something so deeply primal and wild within, pure shakti, the feminine essence of creation.

What I began to notice was an influx of men drawn to my activated shakti, this wild raw primal feminine unlocking within me. They would often say "they wanted to just be around my energy." Now, I had always received male attention, but this was something much deeper and more profound. Men weren't just seeing my pretty face and physique. I could feel that they were drawn to a deeper current of feminine energy that was awakening within me. It was palpable and highly magnetic. As I went deeper into this phase of my life, I began having past-life memories and knowings (gnosis) of a time when all women knew of this power they wielded, and men would visit these women who resided inside beautiful temples, simply to "bask in the presence of their shakti energy." I saw flashbacks and remembered deep in my bones a time when myself and other highly trained sex priestess' would dance in temples, and men would come in full reverence of the divine feminine and worship the current of shakti moving through these women who were merely conduits of the primordial force flowing through their body. As the men would come in and witness a woman in her full erotic essence, he would receive a transmission of shakti himself and it would initiate him into full presence of the moment, where he found a moment of ecstasy and even enlightenment. For several months, I was having vivid visions and visceral memories of these times.

It was knowledge and wisdom beyond my logical mind, and the desire to consciously explore this archetype again in this lifetime became stronger and stronger within me. But because of the stigma of the modern-day "temple dancer" as being a sex worker, I held a lot of fear and resistance around exploring this energy inside of me. And yet, the more I tried to resist it, the more the burning desire inside of me grew, until I eventually had to surrender to what life was guiding me towards.

The reasons I resisted this calling were coming from the parts of myself that were holding power over me. There was so much shame that came up around this archetype, mostly due to how it has been portrayed over the years and expressed in our modern-day culture. She is seen as the whore, the stripper, the sex worker and prostitute, as society suppresses this most powerful and yet sacred archetype. Mary Magdalen was persecuted and exiled for her power and knowing; she was condemned by the church as a sinner and a whore. Women in their fullest sexual expression have been cast deeply into the shadows ever since the story of Lilith. This story and the shame associated with the once-revered temple dancer and sexual healer have cheapened her to something of a second-class citizen in our collective unconscious, as a way to further suppress female sexuality.

This angered and frustrated me because in my visions and dreams of these ancient times, women and the divine feminine were honored and even worshiped for being in their full sexual expression, dancing and healing with their awakened eros flowing freely. It felt so sacred and respectful. I believe strip clubs are the modern-day goddess temples, which was once a place of reverence and worship. However, it is because of all the distortions around sexuality and the collective suppression of the dark feminine that these establishments are now cast into the shadows and often attract more a sleazy vibe and exploitation of feminine eros, versus the true honoring and appreciation of Her in the ancient times. This was something I wanted to rewrite and transform in my own way—through reviving the ancient practices and empowering my own and others' sexuality by reclaiming the dark feminine and healing the split in myself and all those who witnessed me in this expression.

Shakti Sessions

I longed to relive these ancient memories in this lifetime. The desire was so strong that I couldn't ignore it anymore. It started with me offering these men who "wanted to be in the presence of my shakti," to do just that. I knew there had to be an energetic exchange, specifically money, in order to be in my presence. I felt into why these distortions and exploitations of the feminine had taken place, and a lot of it had to do with women not owning their worth and being conditioned to be disempowered and disconnected from money, which was handled for them by club managers/pimps who basically take all their earnings and exploit them. If I was going to explore this, I was going to do it my way, rewriting that story and imprint in the long collective lineage of women who had not owned their worth. Every woman who devalues herself, devalues the entire collective feminine, and every woman who values herself raises the standard and rewrites the story for all women collectively.

I started by offering shakti massage sessions for men from my little cabin in the woods. It was either this or become a stripper on the Gold Coast, which didn't really appeal to the sense of sacredness that I was longing for. I knew I could go in with the purest of intention and alchemise a lot of that dense energy and hold the sacred, but at that stage of my journey I didn't feel ready or strong enough to hold this level of power in order for the men to truly receive to what I was attempting to offer. Plus, I wanted to be in control. I did try and apply to dance at a few clubs, but the universe always got in my way and prevented me from going down that path. Instead it turns out years later, after some core internal lessons had been integrated, was the time I was ready to dance on stage, more on this later. So, at this time in my journey, I followed what was flowing organically, which were my shakti massage sessions.

At the start, I really didn't have much of an idea of what I was doing from a logical perspective, but intuitively, I knew. I would set up my cabin as a beautiful temple space, dim lit with candles, the scent of nag-champa burning, beautiful fabrics and plush pillows and the sounds of a deep bass sexy playlist to curate the overall vibe. We would begin the session facing one another on our plush cushions and start with some basic breathing practices and traditional soul gazing through the left eye, which allowed me to truly see this man in front of me beyond his physical appearance. I would go deeply into his soul and I saw his pain, his fears, his joy, his ecstasy, his desires—it was so profound. It made me sad how many of these men longed to be in true communion with the feminine at this level of depth and intimacy; how they longed to simply be seen by Her. We would then set some intentions and I would understand what his main concerns and desires were, yet I already knew them from looking into his soul. Often, what he said wasn't actually aligned with what I felt was his truth, and it was my job to guide his own knowing back to his truth. Then I would guide him to the massage table and begin the deepest, most sensual massage, worshiping this man in his entirety, both his physical body and through it, his soul.

At this stage of my work with the men, it was just a full-body massage that I offered. No genital massage was offered at all; this only came later in my exploration and development. These initial sessions from my cabin taught me the Lilith art of being in control and holding this erotic space for a man to surrender to my lead, for me to initiate him into truth and depth from simply being seen and witnessed in his desires and truth. It felt like such a gift that I was giving to each and every man, and I was being compensated well for this gift with their financial exchange. I felt the first taste of owning my power, wielding my sexuality and shakti in a way that felt honoring and healing for both parties involved.

In time, I started to go deeper into the dark feminine shadows and explored this archetype even further. After a year in my cabin in the hinterland of Byron Bay, the island of Bali began calling me. An older woman who was one of my mentors at the time invited me to assist her women's tantra retreat in Ubud, Bali. I thought, "Why not?" I knew I wanted to leave Australia and explore the shadow side of what I had opened up in my dark feminine explorations. I had this wild plan to move to Bali and create a new identity and take these sessions to the next level. I can see now why porn stars and strippers create a "stage name." It is a way to externalize this fragmented and demonized archetype within us until we are ready to integrate her as one inside of us. So, it was decided—I booked my one-way ticket to Bali. Things seemed to fall into place divinely. One synchronicity after another occurred. I lived with my mentor for a month and assisted her retreat, learning so much about the dark feminine through her. She challenged me and pushed me to expand, but with love. She was the dark mother I longed for, a guide who could lovingly open me up and take me to the next level of self-inquiry without traumatizing me. She was another one of the teachers that magically appeared in my life, without me seeking her out. I lived with her in this beautiful villa in Bali and experienced what felt like an unofficial apprenticeship, for which I am forever grateful. She saw the potential in me and empowered me to step up. I had never held space for a group bigger than five people and she invited me to support her in holding space for 30 women who were also receiving dark feminine initiations through our week together. I wasn't sure I could do it, but I did—and I received a major upgrade from this experience. I felt like I was being thrown in the deep end and tested to see if I would sink or swim. To go from holding intimate yoga classes with three to five students, to holding space for 30 women experiencing shamanic purging, emotional processing and trauma release—it was a lot, to say the least. And yet I swam. I am so grateful to my mentor for throwing me into this test. I began to believe in myself because she believed in me.

From the retreat, and month long immersion living with this woman, I was now on my own and back on my original mission of exploring more of this dark Lilith sacred prostitute archtype. One day, I walked into one of the popular vegan cafes in Bali and the first man I saw was a well-known shamanic practitioner who I had met briefly back in Australia. I sat down and started chatting with him over our raw vegan salads in classic Bali bowls made out of banana leaves, sipping our dragon fruit smoothies until our mouths were glowing bright pink. I started sharing with him my desires and mission here to explore this dark feminine side of myself and my plans for my sessions, and he just got it. We instantly hit it off and he invited me to come and live with him in the spare room at his villa. Since I was already on a streak of teachers appearing magically in my life and inviting me to live with them, I again thought, "Why not?" Plus, I always wanted to deepen my knowledge of the shamanic arts and he had a beautiful session space and massage table—the perfect place for me to continue my shakti massage sessions.

I moved in the next day and began my explorations. I never advertised my sessions. I wanted to keep it low key and discreet, in such a small community. I would simply go about my day, lounging in the vegan cafes, hopping from spiritual event to spiritual event, and most days I would meet someone who was "drawn to my shakti." From there, I would extend the invitation to come back to my temple space for a "shakti massage session." I just put the offer out there if I felt that I wanted to spend time with the guy, and I could see that his heart and intentions were pure. I was not attached to the outcome but I loved owning my power and offering my gifts, and using this as a real-life training ground. I always gave them a fake name and remained somewhat mysterious, not revealing too much about myself. This was part of the appeal of this mission I was on, exploring my alter-ego seductress dark feminine Lilith archetype, seducing men back to my temple for tantric activations. Once they arrived, I would explain what I do and the finance exchange. Nine times out of 10, every man would choose to stay, and I would take them through the sessions I developed back in Byron Bay. However, it was after the fifth or so man asked me to massage him erotically that the sessions began to change. In that instant, I freaked out and said *No, I don't offer that, get out of here*— and asked him to leave immediately. But then I started thinking... What if I included this in the activation session as a way to support these men in learning how to master their sexual energy? Was there a way to do this that was empowering for me and for them? I had already learned basic tantric massage techniques, specifically Lingam massage as a healing modality and sacred arts practice that, when done right, supported men in learning how to ride the orgasmic wave and overcome things like premature ejaculation, erectile dysfunction and the imprints of sexual traumas.

While I felt called to explore this, naturally, a lot of fears came up, the main one being, *What if people think I'm a prostitute?* Then I realized that what other people think really doesn't matter: this is the archetype I'm here to explore and reclaim in this lifetime— doing so in the healthiest expression, not what we've seen in the exploitations of women's sexuality of previous generations. This archetype holds so much shame in so many women's psyches, and in the collective psyche. Being who I am (a Saggitarius moon and all), I've always been drawn to the taboo and the underbelly of society, for I know these realms hold a lot of power once we liberate the shame associated with them. For whatever reason, in this lifetime I came here to reclaim this archetype in my own unique and empowered way. I offered a few more sessions in the space from Bali, but word was getting around town, and I needed to remain more anonymous if I was going to take my sessions to the next level.

On a steamy hot Sunday in Bali, I was blessed with another synchronicity. After an ecstatic dance class one afternoon, I was sitting on the steps outside the yoga shala, sweaty, heartbroken and crying because the man I was seeing, who was meant to come visit me in Bali from Thailand, had just told me that he was not feeling it was right to come. He shared that intuitively he knew I wasn't in the right space to be with him. And he was right. I had no space for a relationship at this stage of my journey. With all the work I was stepping into with men's sexuality, I was on a secret/not-so-secret mission. So there I was, in tears, when this beautiful man appeared before me and asked me if I was okay. I looked up at him with my puffy eyes and sniffly nose and mumbled something barely coherent, and he just stayed there next to me holding space for me to emote. Once I calmed down, we began conversing and he offered to buy me lunch. I found out that this man was a well-known Advaita Vedanta teacher from Perth, Australia, who was a student of Ramana Maharshi. It made perfect sense, as his energy was just so calming and serene. His presence alone was so healing, capable of soothing me back to good spirits when I was an emotional mess. This man became another key teacher along my journey who just magically appeared. Like the last two teachers, he offered for me to come live with him in his huge house in the Perth Hills, if I ever decided to come to Perth. He also said the house would be available for the next six months. He was heading to India for his annual pilgrimage and offered for me to live there at a ridiculously low price— $100 a week for a four-bedroom home on a large property. I couldn't believe what was happening. I had set the intention to take my tantric work to the next level, and this man comes along and offers me a temple all to myself in the Perth Hills. Plus, I really liked him. He was a sweet and genuine soul, and yet another one of my teachers that I believe was divinely sent to me on my path. I decided to live with him for the month before he left for India, seeing this as an incredible opportunity to also learn from him the teachings of Advaita Vedanta, receiving the transmission simply by being in his presence. If you're not familiar with it, Advaita Vedanta is a Hindu path of spiritual discipline and experience. The term *advaita* (non-duality) refers to the idea that *Brahman* (God) alone is ultimately real, while the transient phenomenal world is an illusory appearance (*maya*) of Brahman. This tradition has many teachings and practices for achieving a state of non-duality.

Men's Tantric Embodiment Sessions

Off I went, with a one-way ticket to Perth, Australia, where it all began—my birth place in this lifetime. I arrived at the beautiful property in the Perth Hills, where the red rich land and the smell of eucalyptus trees invited me deeper into my body and a sense of home. I hadn't been back to my birth place since I was two years old, so it was very powerful to return to this land. The work I was about to embark upon here felt as though it was my second birth of sorts, a rebirth into who I truly came here to be. It was very symbolic to me. In my first month here with this man, who became a mentor of sorts, I learned so much about Advaita Vedanta philosophy and meditation. I also received the masculine fatherly guidance I longed for—yet another fatherly archetype showing up in my life at just the right time—who expanded my consciousness in ways I could never experience on my own. This level of presence and guidance was always what I longed for from my father. Because I never got it from him, I had to seek it out myself in these beautiful male mentors that I was consistently blessed with along my path. The month I spent in Perth became the foundation for me to take my work with men and my own inner alchemy to the next level of power and potency.

Once he left on his annual India pilgrimage, it was time for me to get to work. I updated my website with a new offering, "Men's Tantric Embodiment Sessions." Within one week of updating my website, my website ranked number-one on Google when you searched "Tantra in Perth." I saw this as a major sign that I was on the right path. With zero paid ads or marketing services, my website was on the front page of search results—and not just on the front page, but number-one. Client inquiries came flooding in. My new offerings were an evolution of the shakti sessions I had begun offering in Byron Bay and Bali. I desired to take the men deeper and truly walk the path of the tantric priestess/dakini and initiate these men into higher states of consciousness and sexual healing through their erotic awakening.

At that time, I decided to make a few changes to my initial offering. Now, the men had to go through an initial screening phone interview with me so I could feel that their intentions were aligned before booking them for their sessions. Then, they had to complete a minimum of three sessions of basic fundamental tantra practices such as breathwork, meditation and awareness, inner child work and trauma release work. Only once they had completed these foundational practices, I would take them through a tantric embodiment/tantric massage session, this time, also incorporating lingam massage. Lingam massage is a powerful and healing tantric practice that helps men release trauma from their genitals, and subsequently learn how to ride the orgasmic wave. With specialized breathing techniques, they learn how to circulate their energy throughout their body from the lower centers to the upper centers, which is essentially what's known as sublimation or semen retention. Sublimation is an incredibly healing practice for men, and it's the foundation for a tantric man. It is the process by which he learns how to redirect his sexual energy from the lusty, primal centres into higher levels of consciousness. If a man doesn't redirect this energy from the lower centers of primal instinct, he is essentially operating at an animal level of consciousness. The art of sublimation teaches him how to master his sexual energy rather than being a slave to it by redirecting the energy up the spine for both healing purposes and awakening of higher consciousness. This was my intention with all my sessions.

My new approach was rooted in very traditional practices. I had read stories about the ancient tantrikas who lived in temples and acted as sacred consorts. Young men would spend one to two years training with them, learning how to treat a woman and how to be in the presence of a woman, and also how to refine their own energy. Only after a couple of years would the tantrika teach them the sacred sexual practices. I wanted to honor the traditional ways of the tantric priestesses before me, preparing these men mentally, physically and spiritually before offering them the lingam massage sessions. Of course, a year or more of preparation wasn't realistic, so I adapted the traditional approach and condensed it down to four preliminary sessions. Many of the men would book their sessions with a true desire to learn tantra, specifically wanting to learn how to sublimate their sexual energy.

Because of the way I presented my session page online, and the energy and sacredness with which I held the space of the sessions, I started to find that I attracted only high-caliber men who were serious about doing this deep inner work. I attracted a lot of CEOs and professionals who wanted to learn tantra, overcome premature ejaculation and erectile dysfunctions, heal their relationship with the feminine, become better lovers, and heal sexual traumas. They were longing for a space that was of the caliber and standard I was holding. There were many "tantra massage" parlors and services available in Perth and other parts of Australia, but let's just say they were more of a "rub and tug" type of service. On the other hand, I was truly devoted to this work. If I was going to do it, I was going to do it right. I recruited two other sisters to come live with me and trained them, and we offered sessions together and sometimes solo. We had a strict purification protocol, offering a maximum of four sessions a week so that we could maintain our energetic frequency and rigorously adhere to our practices: meditation, breathwork, yoga, and energy clearing rituals. I don't recall leaving the property much, as my focus was on being a full-time tantric priestess, which involved a lot of energetic alchemy. Because of the level of energy I was working with, I had to do a lot of clearing practices and spend a lot of time alone to restore my energy. I did this for about a year before I fell in love with a man, and the time came where I naturally knew that the karma of this work was complete, and I didn't desire to share my energy with anyone else but my beloved. This chapter closed, and union with one man began.

It was during this experience I was able to deeply dive into embodying the sixth code of the sex priestess: the initiatrix of awakening. It was a code that I remembered on a deep visceral level in my body from many past lives. I felt that I released light years of karma through letting go of fear, guilt and shame around my sexuality and consciously exploring and liberating the sacred prostitute archetype. To be clear, this never involved having sexual intercourse with anyone. My sessions ended at lingam massage, with me fully clothed the entire time. I was very clear on this important piece and it is a part of what made the work so sacred and empowering for both parties. It was by liberating this energy that had been so stigmatized inside me, and exploring it in a safe way that felt right, that I truly came home to my sexual power.

When we liberate those parts of ourselves that we once shamed ourselves for—the parts that society shames us for and others shame us for—we truly come into our power. In a way, this was the final healing around my sexual abuse: taking the power back into my own hands and refusing to suppress my natural and innocent desires that were robbed of me in my childhood. Being the tantric priestess gave me a second chance to explore and play out my deepest erotic desires, on my own terms. I was in control this time. For this reason, I can now see it as an incredibly healing part of my journey to sexual liberation. I am not saying that every person who has been sexually abused should go down this same path. What I am saying is that your deepest desires and the whispers of your soul are gateways into the unconscious. Several years later, I would return to my deepest desires to unlock another level of my journey as the initiatrix.

Becoming Isis

My return home to Australia this past year proved to be the final leg of this tantric heroine's journey I've been on. I finally felt ready to integrate my dark feminine in the way I had most longed to explore her: exotic dancing.

It seems as though the dark feminine likes to make an appearance at the start of my seven-year cycles. This time she came right on cue, just after my 35th birthday.

When she made her latest appearance, the urge to dance in gentleman's clubs became so strong that I could not resist. The opportunity to do so came along organically and effortlessly, so I knew the time was right.

Nadine Lee

It was in my early 20s that I first felt the desire to explore exotic dancing. But at that time in my life, I do not feel that I would have been able to hold the energy required for this role. As the club manager consistently assured me on my first night, *You need a thick skin to survive here.* I can see now that I needed to experience certain initiations before I stepped foot in my eight-inch pleaser high heels in this dark and seductive gentleman's club on the Gold Coast.

My intention for doing this was not for money. Rather, I was interested purely in self-exploration and the deepening of my embodied experience of the sex priestess archetype. Specifically, I wanted to truly liberate my dark feminine who longed to be witnessed in her fullest erotic expression, dancing on a stage as a conduit for eros to move through her body temple.

Texting back and forth with the club manager, I was nervous and excited as I was figuring out where to find my outfits and deciding on my stage name. At first I said my name would be Nadia, but then recalled that name as it felt too similar to my real name. I then suggested Venus, to which she said, *We already have a Venus.* I proposed Lalita, to which she responded, *Please make it something men can remember if they are drunk.* But I wasn't going to dull my name down for anyone—it was too important. My stage name was the energy of the archetype I was evoking during this exploration! *Okay,* I told her. *Isis. My stage name is going to be Isis.* I figured if I was going to explore a deepening of the sex priestess archetype, I would evoke the OG Sex Priestess herself: Isis, the Egyption goddess of magic, who could resurrect the dead and turn princes into kings. Isis, the leader of the Cult of Isis, a group of highly trained tantrikas and sex priestesses—women trained in the erotic arts. That was the frequency I was going to anchor during this exploration.

Isis it was.

Sex Priestess

Every time I would meet a gentleman and introduce myself as Isis, he would either respond with intrigue, saying something along the lines of, *Ohhhh the Egyptian Goddess, I am a history buff, I know,* or with ignorance, *Oh Isis, like the terrorist group?* Their response to the name alone weeded out the ones who were ready to receive the sex priestess initiation or not. I actually believe that the distortion of her name as being identified with a terrorist group is yet another way to suppress feminine power and associate it with fear and resistance. This gave me a good glimpse into their level of brainwashing and receptivity to the energy I was bringing.

I worked a total of three nights at the club over a span of three weeks. My time here was nothing short of incredible. To enter this world from a place of awareness and intentionality was profound. From the first moment I stepped up on that stage in my eight-inch heels, commanding the attention of countless men whose eyes were laser-focused upon me, it felt so familiar, so right and so powerful. I felt as if I was picking up where I left off in many previous lifetimes as a temple dancer, performer and sex priestess in her fullest expression. When I would move my body and undulate pure life force energy and pleasure through my body, I felt that I was evoking something so deep in every man who witnessed me. The difference between myself and a lot of exotic dancers is that I was truly embodied in my pleasure. There was not one ounce of doing this for attention or validation. It was purely the joy of feeling so turned on and activated in my pleasure body. Being witnessed in that just invited me deeper into my fullest expression. It was as if my pleasure evoked the men's presence, and their presence invited me deeper into my embodied experience.

Presence and Pleasure

This expression of men witnessing a woman dance in her eros is such a beautiful metaphor for the dance between masculine and feminine in life. How deeply can a man hold presence and a safe space for her to express her fullness and beauty? She overflows with the gifts of feminine radiance as a result of his presence, and he receives those blessings and gifts. He then gifts her more of the presence, protection and provision she desires. This was my experience being witnessed on that stage.

Offering private dances with the men in the champagne rooms, I witnessed and embodied even more deeply the power of feminine eros and its ability to invite a man into deeper presence and power. Their eyes glued on me, the men would go into a trance-like meditative state that brought me deep joy. This is the power of the feminine. Her body is a transmitter of pleasure and eros; pure life force that invites a man into a moment of *samadhi*, of sheer enlightenment. All thoughts cease to exist and he is met in the moment of nothingness, the void. This is something that yogis and monks train endlessly for, and it can be evoked in a moment of gazing at the female form. (Interestly, the Buddha became enlightened after battling Mara, his inner demons, all night—but that the moment of his awakening happened as he was gazing at the morning star, Venus. A moment of gazing at the feminine!). As I would seduce them deeper and deeper into presence through my body, I would then teach them how to breathe properly and hold eye contact with me. It was such a gift to offer these tantric teachings to men who may never have experienced them otherwise.

Surprisingly enough, once I had fully derobed, most of the gentlemen simply wanted to talk to me. Their eros had been evoked, and through me guiding their breath and awareness, we actively moved the eros up into the heart and throat. Nine times out of ten, they simply wanted to be heard. I ended up being booked for hours. Once derobed, I would slide my silk kimono back on and sit by their side and become their therapist. This reminded me of my shakti sessions from years before. At their core, all men deeply desire connection, and they want to be seen and heard. Even the club manager and the seasoned exotic dancers at the club told me this on the first night. They said, *Looks are useful here, but they aren't everything. What helps you here is if you have a brain and can hold a decent conversation.* Taking this advice, each night I ended up in the top 3% of earners among the women. I believe it is because I genuinely enjoyed this experience, gave it my all and was doing it for my own pleasure.

My final night dancing at the club, I knew I had got what I came for. I had integrated the lessons of my dark feminine, and now the final lesson was deciding when to leave, on my own terms. I had countless *dejavu* moments in that club, memories of doing this type of work in past lives out of obligation and necessity to survive, not from the purest intention. In this lifetime, I got clear guidance about returning to the club/temple and saying *no* when I'd had enough. When I left that night, I felt that I had cleared lifetimes of karma from myself and my family lineage. As I walked out the door of the gentlemen's club, my energetic signature said: *This lifetime is not about doing anything out of obligation, especially not selling my sexuality.* I rewrote the script completely and shared my sexuality only in an empowering and liberating way.

Awakening Through Your Feminine Eros

To become the initiatrix, you must first fully activate your own desire and eros. Think about your own desires, your relationship to your own sexuality and how you share your eros with others, especially men. It could be similar to mine or more likely something completely different! For this code, I invite you into self-reflection with the following questions:

- What's your relationship to your own sexuality?
- What parts of your sexuality are you too embarrassed to own?
- What are some of your deepest sexual fantasies, taboos, fetishes?
- What parts of yourself do you feel will be rejected by others, especially men?
- What erotic archetype do you hold judgment over? How can you explore this archetype in order to release the judgment you may be holding inside of yourself?

During my exploration phase, I truly embodied and understood the power of female sexuality and eros. I experienced how we are the initiates of tantric energy, and when used intentionally, can yield deeply awakening experiences in men with our presence alone. I think this was the most important piece of my experience: understanding that feminine presence alone is the gift and the initiator of male eros. This is because feminine energy is the force of creation itself. The way it moves, spirals and dances throughout all of creation is pure beauty and art. This force seduces us into a deeper presence and more awakened engagement with life. This is the role of the true seductress: she is the fully sexually liberated feminine expressing itself through a woman's body. She invites everyone in her path into full presence, even if only for a moment—a moment of being truly free of the mind, a moment of bliss, a moment of awakening. Even from the early days men "just wanted to be in my presence." I didn't have to do anything. Sexual acts or physical touch didn't even need to be involved. I invite you to begin to notice the impact your presence alone has on the men around you. Taking out any sexual act or energy, you will notice simply that your energy deeply impacts a man. He responds to you with his body language, his words, and his level of presence. Your mere being can invite him into a deeper presence and draw him out of his frantic headspace into a dropped-in space inside his own body. This happens simply through you being deeply connected to your own body.

It is the pure *shakti* that is pulsing through every woman by virtue of her being a woman that is so alluring, so enticing and liberating for all who come into her presence—men and women. Women at an earlier stage of their journey who come into the presence of a fully sexually awakened woman receive a transmission about the deep feminine potential within them. This gives them permission to explore and unlock their own eros.

Ask any stripper or sex worker about their experiences. A lot of men come to them simply to talk and be in the presence of an embodied woman. Often the men aren't even looking for sex or physical touch. This was my experience diving into these worlds of exotic dancing and offering the tantric massage sessions. Here I learned so much that surprised me about men, especially in the gentlemans club. Once they saw my naked body–they just wanted to talk and have someone to gently stroke their hair with loving devotion and tenderness as I listened to them share about everything from their children, their former marriage or divorce, their businesses. It was a fascinating exploration into the male psyche. Yes, men were coming for the healing and learning, but often they wanted to just be witnessed in their truth, sharing their deepest fears, desires, and vulnerabilities. This gave me such a deeper compassion for men. I quickly saw that so many of them think they want the sexual connection, but at their core, what they are longing for is simply human intimacy and the loving and nurturing presence of the feminine. This experience allowed me to release judgment over the nature of male sexuality, which was a big part of helping me to forgive my abuser on a deeper level.

Becoming The Initiatrix

You might be wondering how you can integrate and embody the initiatrix of awakening without becoming an exotic dancer or offering tantric massage sessions. I want to share that going down these avenues is absolutely not required for you to embody this code. For me personally, this is where my path led me. In sharing these experiences of listening to the deep desires within me, I offer an invitation for you to listen to what deep erotic desires are bubbling within you—because these desires offer the key to your initiatory gifts. Beyond the healing and transforming power of your presence, there are deeper gifts to be found within your own dark feminine.

As I've said, the most important way you can be a healing and awakening force for others is through the power of your presence. The dark feminine archetype expresses through every woman in her own unique flavor according to what core soul curriculum she signed up for in this lifetime. It's important to first ask yourself, *What are some of your deepest desires around your own sexuality? Where do you feel your edge is? Which parts of you do you most shame in yourself and others?* The answers to these questions are good indications of where your dark feminine is inviting you. Honoring our desires is what liberates us. It frees up so much stuck energy in the body and therefore allows for that free flow of eros or shakti to move through us as the energy and archetype of the initiatrix of awakening itself. If we are holding onto all this stuck shame and guilt, we aren't living fully expressed, and our capacity to support and inspire others is much more limited. The first key is to identify where those blockages are within you that long to be expressed and thus liberated.

Once you have fully liberated yourself through liberating your sexuality, then you step onto the path of initiating others. For example, if I were to jump up on that stage in the gentleman's club with all sorts of insecurities around my body, disengaged from the experience and feeling zero pleasure but rather shame in my body—the impact I would have on those men would not be the same as it is when I am feeling so empowered, embodied and in my sexual sovereignty. This is a metaphor for life. Life is the stage. How are you showing up? What kind of energy are you bringing to your relationships, your projects, your everyday activities? What kind of responses are you getting? The core of this code is to look at those final parts of yourself that are holding you back from being fully present in your body and from being fully comfortable in expressing yourself and your sexuality—for you and you alone. Most of the work we have done prior to this chapter has been the invitation for you to do this deep inner work. Once you are free of these shackles of shame, guilt and fear, you can finally liberate others from their own shackles of shame, guilt and fear or anything else that is blocking them from being fully present to love—love which knows no obstructions.

As it turned out, for me, working with men was the catalyst for another type of initiation: taking my work with women to the next level. I realized that although this work initiating men was important, I didn't just want to be doing this work on my own. I wanted all women in the world to be able to offer to their partners what I was offering my clients, which I believed would cultivate more intimacy and love on this planet through sacred relationships and sacred union. When women are sexually awakened and sovereign, they lead the way for all of humanity— and it starts with the men in their life. I knew I had to get back to working with women. I wanted to teach women how to liberate their own sexuality and heal their sexual traumas, just like I had—so they could show up in their relationships as the sex priestess and integrate her into their lives and this world, beyond the ancient temples, which leads us to our final code: Living as the Sex Priestess.

CODE 7:
LIVING AS THE SEX PRIESTESS

Sex Priestess

You're probably familiar with the hero's journey of countless myths and stories: the hero or heroine gets the initial call to action, goes off on a journey and leaves everything they've known behind, learning all their key soul lessons along the way, only to find themselves ultimately returning back to where they started from. The hero completes the journey by sharing the wisdom they've accumulated with the community they left at the outset of their journey.

This timeless story arc is symbolic of the soul's journey. Like the hero, we go off on journeys and have these peak experiences, in ceremony, on retreats, or on our yoga mat—but the true spiritual task is to integrate all the lessons from these peak experiences into everyday life. This is the whole point of the "healing path." It is not a self-indulgent path to fixate on forever, constantly seeking higher and higher states of consciousness and bliss. There must come a time when you share with others the fruits of your labor, however that might look to you. This is when life becomes the ritual or ceremony.

This code, and the work of integrating the sex priestess into everyday life, is about discovering the secret that a sex priestess is in essence an awakened, empowered wholesome woman. She has answered the soul call to heal herself, to look at her sexual shadows, to reclaim those exiled parts of her, to face her core wounds, and find her power through this process. She goes on a wild journey, gaining so much wisdom along her path—only to find herself back where it all began. And yet, she is different. The lens through which she perceives the world has shifted radically as her internal world has come to a place of peace, wholeness and integration. From this place she finds her power. She extends her wisdom outwards by supporting others along their own soul's journey using her own unique gifts and wisdom.

Nadine Lee

As I write this chapter, the divine unfolding of life has found me returning to my hometown in Australia after being away for nearly three years. This indeed is my return home, a full-circle integration, after what feels like years of running. Growing up, I could not wait to escape my situation, from the emotional abuse I experienced in our family environment and the pain of having to face my sexual abuser frequently at family gatherings. When I finally found spirituality, I felt that I had found my escape route. I felt I had made it out, but the patterns I was running from would resurface in all kinds of different ways in my reality. Over the years, every time I would visit my family, the cycle of pain and trauma would play out again, and I would end up running back to wherever I had escaped to at the time—Bali, Mexico, Costa Rica, LA. The thing I have learned is this: the more we run away from the source of our pain, the more amplified it becomes. As they say, "wherever you go, there you are." Our "stuff" follows us everywhere. In every community, I would notice archetypes that resembled my abuser, my mother and my father. It became so predictable that it was almost comical. After I would settle into a new community: *Oh yep there is my father archetype; Yep, there's the abuser; Yep, there is my mother.* In every single damn community, in people I met all over the world, my mirrors would show up for me to have the opportunity to face what I had been running from—the source of my pain. The universe is clever like that. It isn't going to let us get off scotch-free from our evolution by avoiding facing our core relational wounds.

Sometimes, however, physical, mental and/or energetic space is absolutely needed from the perpetrators or cause of deep pain. For me, creating this massive distance by fleeing the country for many years was incredibly healing and an incredibly important stage of my journey. It was a way for me to finally state my boundaries, which was a whole new language I had to learn the hard way. I do believe that drastic measures like this are sometimes necessary, especially if you have had any form of abuse (and sexual abuse in particular, which, as I explained in earlier chapters, blurs your entire sense of boundaries). Leaving home, by being able to put up a huge boundary between you and the source of your pain—the abusers or people involved—is needed. However, eventually the day will come where you can face them again with all the lessons accumulated on your path and find true freedom, for the old triggers no longer arise as you find the trauma has been cleared. Ram Dass said, "If you think you are enlightened, go spend a week with your family." This is because the family is where most of our pain stems from. In fact, all our wounds are mostly relational and they all begin in the biological family.

I used to think that escaping to places like India and Bali, living in ashrams and spiritual communities, was going to advance me spiritually. I thought that the only place I could feel connected to spirit and my true self was in these traditional spiritual settings. The thing I learned is that when we place anything outside of ourselves (for example, *I need to go to India to feel spiritual* or *I need to take psychedelics to have a spiritual experience*), we are missing the point. We are giving away all of our power—not to mention our innate connection to the divine—to an external circumstance. This is a common misconception along the path as we begin our ascension journey. However, what I have learned along my own heroine's journey and embodiment of the sex priestess—the integrated woman—is that everything and everywhere is spiritual. Being in the thick of suburbia is no less spiritual than meditating in an ashram in India. (Another cosmic joke I had to realize!) I believe when we embody the sex priestess is when we begin to embody this truth, for we are integrated in both Sex and Spirit. When we unlock Code 7, we begin to find the sacred in the mundane.

Finding Our Way Back Home

A mentor of mine introduced me to the concept of the omega symbol—a circle that is open at the bottom, with two straight lines on either side—as a representation of the hero's journey, or the peak experience. It is as if you are walking along a straight line in your life, and then something happens (a catalyst or awakening moment) and you are catapulted up out of your everyday reality. You learn all these new and exciting things, your old identity starts to get replaced by your new spiritual identity, and everything is so shiny and new. This is the ascension process, which I see as the *Priestess* aspect of the sex priestess. This eventually comes to a peak, at the top of the omega symbol. Then eventually, what goes up must come down. The next phase of the journey is the *descension* process, which I see as the *Sex* aspect of the sex priestess. This is where you must begin to actually embody everything you learned on the upward ascension spiral. You come back into inhabit the body and draw spirit into sex; into matter. You must learn to go beyond concepts and actually start embodying or living what you learned in books, workshops, theories and spiritual experiences. This descension process is often painful, because it means we have to feel whatever emotions are still there residing in the body, along with what feels like our fall from grace, bliss, love and light bubbles.

Once we have integrated our lessons on an embodied, grounded level, we return back along that original path that we began on, but this time, we're a quantum leap ahead. We have a whole new perspective and outlook on life that allows us to truly live integrated in our spiritual and material lives. There is no split. This is similar to the way that we often search all our lives for love, happiness, contentment outside of ourselves in all the wrong places, only to realize that we've forgotten to look in the most obvious place—inside of ourselves. Eventually we always wind up where we left off, coming back home to ourselves. It's almost like some sort of cosmic joke our egos play on us. They lead us to the ends of the earth, only to realize that what we were searching for was with us all along. But it wasn't for nothing. The journey had to be taken. This is the whole point of this human-spiritual experience. The sex priestess is the middle point of this omega symbol, for it is the ultimate representation of embodying the balance and integration, through merging sex and spirit within us.

The sex priestess is what we would call an illuminated one, a spiritual guide and teacher. However, she is not interested in positioning herself as a guru, for she is an everyday woman humbly walking amongst us all, initiating awakening in and through all she infuses her heart and soul into. She has fully remembered her purpose and why she came here in this incarnation, to facilitate awakening and remembrance. She has walked this path and can now guide others who walk behind her. The sex priestess is unstoppable and unapologetic about what feels right and true for the greatest good of all humanity and her soul's evolution, for she will not hold back in speaking truth and calling out truth wherever it needed. The sex priestess knows how to use her healing love merged with her sexual energy by radiating it through her body as the transmission. She *is* the transmission. She swims in a sea of authenticity and is lit from within. When you meet her and look into her eyes, you know that you are these things, too. She reminds you of who you truly are. She reignites your flames of eros and guides you to burn away all that is not true so that your illuminated heart and consciousness can shine through. You will walk away forever changed by simply a glance from her into the depths of your soul.

As you've experienced throughout the journey of this book, the path of living the sex priestess is a journey of alchemising sexual trauma into sexual liberation. It is about turning our greatest source of pain into our greatest source of power as we move from victim to victor. Whether you endured sexual abuse or not in this lifetime, as a woman you carry the generational and collective trauma of all women around our sexuality. And it's not only sexual trauma; the sex priestess knows how to alchemize any pain into wisdom and compassion. We all have a story, we all have a core wound that we are afraid to face, that we may still be allowing to define us. Facing and healing this wound is the heroine's journey, and this has indeed been my own journey in life. If you are reading this book, I believe that you are here for this exact same reason: to remember your power and to realize you are not a victim of your circumstances, your past or whatever has happened to you. This book is a transmission to inspire you to live a life beyond your story and turn it into your art, your compassion and ultimately the passion that fuels your dharma. It is a journey of remembering the truth—that you are love— and releasing the old story and the past experiences through facing them head on, taking a journey into the underworld into the depths of the unconscious and being willing to face off with your inner demons. When we finally find the courage to face the shame, the guilt, the fear, the control, we become fearless, for we stop running and are finally able to live from full presence and power. When we cultivate this presence, an inner silence emerges which is the medium of the light within us. In cultivating this inner silence we create a space in which our light can shine, and this light nourishes and illuminates the path for others. In this realization of the infinite dimensionality of her true nature, there can no longer be any fear, no longer any sense of anything missing, because one is all and nothing.

Stepping Into Your Dharma

Through this journey of shedding our old skin, stripping it down to the core of our inner light and embodying the sex priestess, the question is now, *What did I come here to do?* It's amazing how we come here from source, as pure beings of innocence, unconditional love and trust—only to have all these conditions placed upon us that are not ours, all these traumas inflicted upon us that were not our choice and that cloud us from our true essence of pure innocence, love and trust. These experiences place layers of old skin over us that over time create a hardened shell that blocks our inner light from emerging. It is the unraveling of these layers of old skins that brings us back to the truth again. When we arrive back at this place, it doesn't mean that we're suddenly enlightened and have everything figured out. It is now about asking the real questions: *Who am I? What do I want to create? How am I meant to serve?*

We ask these questions from a place of clarity, deep overflowing service and a clear creative channel. It is a path of remembrance versus seeking. This is the path of tantra. First we focus on purification and clearing the old emotional debris caused by traumas, then comes the activation of the sexual energy, which is the ignition of the fires within and then, and only then it is time to create with this powerful force of creation and serve from a clear, open vessel. From Codes 5 to 7, we've taken a journey from co-creating our desires to becoming a healing presence for others to remembering why we came here and accepting the mission ahead.

Living the sex priestess is about being that embodiment of truth of love and radiant life force energy pulsing through you. It is asking yourself, *Now that I have healed myself, how can I be of service to others? What is it I came here to create? What wants to birth through me?* Living the sex priestess is now about true sexual liberation. When I speak about sexual liberation, I am not solely referring to being a better lover and having great sex (but of course that happens!). In my eyes, when you are sexually liberated, walking the path of the sex priestess, every part of you liberates. Every part of you unleashes its fullest potential.

If there are dysfunctions or lingering stagnant emotions in your sexuality, this blocks your very life force from free flowing.

Shame is the number-one emotion that we store around our sexual experiences, around our very relationships to our bodies. Shame is the lowest vibrational frequency we can be in. So when you liberate yourself from the shackles of shame—the number-one emotion that blocks your sexuality and your relationship with your body—you are free. There is so much shame that others impose upon us (traumas, societal, governments, religions, schooling systems) around our sexuality, which cuts us off from our very source of power. When you release shame, you are liberated. You no longer live according to what society expects of you. You no longer choose partners based on who you think you should be with. You are no longer a slave to a system designed to suppress you in every way.

Becoming sexually liberated means living a life in alignment with our deepest truths because we no longer hold shame around our very existence. This is when you start living your dharma, your true essence and fulfilling your soul's purpose in this lifetime.

As I shared earlier, I never set out to teach what I teach now. In fact, I heavily resisted it and had zero interest in walking this path. But as soon as I stopped resisting what was naturally unfolding in my life, let go and let God handle it, literally—the answers to what I came here to do were so obvious. The biggest hurdle I had to overcome to answer my soul calling was letting go of who I thought I was, and who I was conditioned to be, by my family, the education system, my friend circle and the community at large. There was a deep shame I had to work through to own that my soul was calling me towards a path that wasn't exactly conventional. I certainly wasn't going to study to become a lawyer or accountant. Walking away from my life as I knew it was painful, but I knew that the pain of staying in that situation and life compromising my deepest soul's truth and longing would be far more painful. The pain of the initial letting go was worth it. When we let go of what is not aligned for us any longer, it creates space for so much to enter our lives which is far more aligned with what is true inside of us.

It really is this simple. So many people struggle with finding their purpose in life. It gets a lot of people very upset and confused, feeling as though they are wasting their life and living a life of inauthenticity, or somehow failing to actualize their potential. And yet, the answers are usually staring them directly in their face. Maybe you can relate to this too. It is often a matter of just getting out of our own way and letting go of who we think we are and what others expect of us, and turning our attention inward. We have to stop listening to everyone around us and begin listening to the most important voice—the one inside of us. The path I have uniquely walked shapes everything I teach now. Everything in my life is a part of my dharma and contributes to what I am ultimately here to offer, including the most painful things. The incidents that seemed at the time like they would haunt me and cause lifelong damage, such as the sexual abuse, turned out to be my greatest teachers. Through my own healing journey, they turned out to be part of my soul's curriculum in this lifetime to heal myself and help others overcome sexual abuse/trauma and turn it into power.

Take a moment right now and reflect on some of the adversities you've faced in your life—the journey that only you have walked in this lifetime. This is a good indication of where to begin looking to uncover your dharma or soul's purpose.

Uncovering your dharma or soul's purpose is understanding that your soul experiences hold a unique code and that this is the essence of your offering and gifts to the world. You are living your dharma when you begin to embody the lessons integrated from your unique heroine's journey that have shaped who you've become, and learn how to radiate this as the essence of your offerings. This is when you can begin to serve from depth, integrity and authenticity, however that may look. For every single person it looks completely different. Your job is to dive so deep inside of yourself to find what feels most authentic and true for you. Only you know this.

Cracking Your Unique Code

Code 7 is about cracking your own unique code containing your essence, gifts and dharmic path in this lifetime. It is here that you come to truly own and embody the unique and precious codes that only you embody.

Your codes are *everything*. You could say these codes are the masculine pillar of consciousness behind your life, infused into every creation manifestation (feminine). When you are clear on your unique codes that only you embody, you naturally exude more confidence, clients and customers can be magnetized to you more easily, and there is a clarity which is infused into all your offerings. This creates a solid foundation for your feminine creativity to birth from. There is only one of you, and only one of you who came here to do what you uniquely do. I have worked with hundreds of women over the past decade, helping them uncover their unique gifts and step into the role that life calls them into. Many of the women I have helped in this arena are deeply passionate about sacred union, restoring harmony between their inner masculine and feminine and supporting others to do the same, as individuals and in partnership. Many of my clients are also deeply inspired to share the sacred sexuality teachings and awaken the eros in women on the planet, creating spaces for them to take back their power through reclaiming their sexuality. And there have been many of my clients who are passionate about supporting women step into financial freedom through coaching them around their money blocks. Women often come to me with a knowing of what they came here to do, yet they are still holding onto fear of putting themselves out there and truly stepping onto their path. Something holds them back from claiming, "This is what I came here to do." Our work together, healing and unleashing their sacred sexuality, frees up so much energy tied up in shame, fear and guilt, literally releasing it through the body, which they can then apply to living their true purpose. I always say the keys to unlocking your power and gifts is through your body, specifically through your yoni and womb, because it is here that we hold so much stuck stagnant energy, that blocks us from expressing ourselves, being in our power and unleashing our creativity.

Through this process, you must remember that there is no competition when it comes to living your truth and expressing your soul's gifts—what you came here to do is unique. When you realize this, there is no such thing as comparison. For example, if both you and I are teaching feminine embodiment, the way you express and teach it will be completely different from me. Why? Because my soul has gone through a unique series of initiations and experiences that are distinct from yours. I always share this with my clients and students because many people hold the limiting belief that there is "not enough room for me." This leads us to do a real disservice to humanity by holding back our gifts to the world. Everyone came here with a unique piece of the puzzle, and when everyone is living in their fully expressed selves, we all contribute to the entire puzzle and we complete it together. Your piece is a critical piece, and if you don't fulfill it in this lifetime, whatever it may be, however it may look, you are letting down others, too. The thing is, when you unlock your code, you also help others unlock theirs. It's like you've lit the candle inside yourself and that flame helps the person next to you light their flame—and the ripple effect goes on. When you awaken, you help all awaken. Just imagine right now, waking up on your deathbed and realizing you never fulfilled your soul's purpose—what a waste of a life that would be. It is never too late to begin, either. My own mother fulfilled her dream of becoming a nurse, returning to university to complete her undergraduate degree in nursing at the age of 60! This is just one example. It's never too late to fulfill your dreams and live your soul's calling.

Getting clear on your unique code begins with reflecting upon a multitude of elements and experiences in your life, including:

1. Your unique life experiences
2. The soul imprints you have come in with from previous lifetimes (aka, what you naturally embody)
3. What you naturally activate in other people and have done so for your entire life
4. What comes naturally to you

You've seen how I've drawn upon my own unique life experiences, the trials and tribulations I had overcome in my childhood trauma and abuse, all the way to my past-life memories as a tantric temple dancer, and to the present day, being consistently told by others that I activate their eroticism and something deep inside of them, like a blade of truth or a mirror shining back to them their power. I have also always been a really great listener and counsel. From as early as I can recall, I was counseling everyone in my close proximity, including my own mother through her marital issues (not ideal, but it gave me excellent relationship coaching skills). I was always the sounding board for all my friends, giving the best advice and often simply just holding space for them to emote or express so that they could naturally come to their own conclusions. Never did I think I could make listening to people a career, but turns out that is a huge part of what I do now. I also love writing, and always have, so to write this book is a deeper fulfillment of my dharma.

I invite you to think back to all the things that come naturally and effortlessly to you. Your dharma is a combination of what you are naturally good at, what you enjoy, what difficulties you have overcome, and what is in your soul's destiny. A really good place to start thinking about: *What is it that excites you the most?* Amplify more of that in your life. "Finding your purpose" really doesn't have to be a complicated process. Rather, it's just becoming more of who you truly are and letting that shine through whatever you do. And remember that the most powerful thing about the sex priestess is not what she does but her quality of *being*. Who you are is much more important than what you do, and what you do should flow naturally from your beingness.

Next, take some time to make your way through the following journaling prompts to gain deeper clarity around your soul's purpose and your unique codes.

Self-inquiry Journal Prompts

- Reflect upon your life journey: Where have you come from? What adversities have you overcome? What has supported you in getting to where you are today?
- Past life codes: What memories do you have from past lives? Do you remember doing any ancient practices? What power portals are you naturally drawn to on this planet? What sense do you have of deeper embodied wisdom that comes from lifetimes beyond this one?
- What modalities and teachings have most impacted you along your path?
- When you have gone through your dark night(s) of the soul, what has truly helped you see the light and

alchemise your pain into your power and newfound wisdom?
- What truly motivates you? What excites you the most?
- Reflect back to your childhood, what did you know you were here to do? What games did you play and what has always come naturally to you?
- This week, message 5-10 of your closest friends from different areas of your life, and ask them: *What do I activate or inspire in you when you are around me?*

END NOTE

Never forget, dear reader: this is a spiralic journey. Now that you've completed your first voyage through the seven codes, you will find yourself coming back to them many times, often unexpectedly and rarely in order, as you activate deeper and deeper layers of your own essence and wisdom. The important thing is to say yes to yourself—to make a lifelong commitment to your own journey and process. Answer the call to your own healing and empowerment, again and again. Say yes. Reclaim your shadow parts, face your wounds, liberate yourself. Walk the path of the sex priestess and you will find that the Goddess, always, will walk by your side.

Many blessings on the journey,
Nadine

RESOURCES/ APPENDIX

BOOKS

The Magdalen Manuscript: The Alchemies of Horus & the Sex Magic of Isis by Tom Kenyon

shorturl.at/bsz14

COURSES

Halo Sorenko Shakti Temple Arts
https://www.shaktitemplearts.com/

The Creatress Online Course
https://tantricalchemy.net/the-creatress/

Pleasure Principles Online Course
https://tantricalchemy.net/courses/pleasure-principles/

Sexual Alchemy for Men Online Course
https://tantricalchemy.net/courses/sexual-alchemy-for-men/

PRODUCTS

Jade Eggs & Yoni Wands
https://www.tantricalchemy.net/yoni-crystals

Notes

Notes

Notes

Notes

Notes

Printed in Great Britain
by Amazon